# ADVENTURE IN ADVERSITY

Paul E. Billheimer

Tyndale House
Publishers, Inc.
Wheaton, Illinois

First printing, March 1984

Library of Congress Catalog Card Number 83-51174
ISBN 0-8423-0034-1, paper

Printed in the United States of America

*Adventure in Adversity*

## CONTENTS

## ONE
# AN INTRODUCTION TO ADVERSITY

### ADVERSITY IS PURPOSEFUL

If affliction does not come with a message from the heart of God, as Alexander Maclaren believes, then it has to be accidental and wholly without meaning. *One of the principal lessons in the Book of Job is that adversity is neither accidental nor meaningless.* Through Job God is telling us that adversity is purposeful and that purpose is good. Illustrating Romans 8:28, it verifies the truth that every affliction of the righteous is intended to be educational. Therefore, if properly accepted, it is good and not evil. Although it comes from Satan, it comes with God's permission. Satan is a created being. He functions only by power originating in God. He could not move an eyelash without the Creator's energy. Satan intends his affliction for evil, but God intends it for good. Therefore, the most important thing is not to get rid of it as soon as possible. The most crucial thing is to understand that it has an important message and to be humble enough to receive the instruction. Then faith for healing or deliverance could come easily. Only then is one ready to sing, "Only Believe." *Until we are meek enough and have enough faith to hear God's voice, learn the new lesson, and make the necessary adjustment, faith for healing and deliverance may be delayed.*

ONE NEGLECTED AREA

You may spend much time in prayer for your deliverance; you may strive to exercise faith; you may be anointed and prayed for by the most gifted person without apparent success. But when you get really quiet enough to hear God's voice, come into the new revelation God has for you, and make the confession or adjustment God desires, *you may find faith coming spontaneously.* Perhaps God does not work this way in every case. One cannot force God into a mold. He is sovereign. But this is one of the lessons to be learned from Job. This apparently was the view of Watchman Nee when he said, "We seldom learn anything new about God except through adversity." *This is a neglected area in some of our teaching.*

A PERFECT THEOLOGY FOR HEALING

We are taught that all sickness is from the devil, and that is true. We are told that the atonement covers the entire scope of human need, and that is also true. We remember that "by His stripes we were healed," and we are convinced of this. It is emphasized that Jesus paid the full price for our deliverance 2,000 years ago and that He has done all that He ever will do to provide for our liberation. We are reminded that Jesus never turned anyone away but healed all who came to Him. We are assured that miracles of healing were abundant in the early church and that the early church was

God's prototype for the entire age. *We are persuaded that all of this is true. We believe that the Bible is a perfect theology for healing of the entire person.*

TRUTH HAS MORE THAN ONE DIMENSION

All of the foregoing is accepted. But is it the whole, the entire truth? Is it the full-orbed truth? Many Bible students agree that divine truth is many-sided, that it has more than one dimension. Sometimes one essential dimension is ignored. The Book of Job supports this conviction.

*Alexander Maclaren says that every affliction comes with a message from the heart of God.* This is either true or false. If we say that it is false, we affirm that affliction is accidental and therefore without meaning. *This leaves one drifting on a sea of chance, without a guiding chart or compass.*

AFFLICTION PURPOSEFUL

I believe the Book of Job teaches otherwise, revealing that Satan is the source of adversity but that even Satan is under God's control. He can do nothing without God's permission. Read the first chapter of Job for yourself. It also reveals that all affliction of believers is purposeful and when properly accepted is educational. If Job had attended a modern healing service and been healed the first night, he might have missed an indispensable revelation of God. *Nothing is as eternally important as a new revelation of God. Believe it or not, that is more important than receiving your healing.* Growing, divine illumination will be our thrilling experience throughout eternity. *An ever-increasing revelation of God is the ultimate glory.* Had Job been healed without receiving that new insight, it would have been an inestimable loss to him and to us, possibly even an eternal loss.

## VALUE OF ADVERSITY

If Watchman Nee is correct in saying that we never learn anything new about God except through adversity, should we not thank God for the adversity? To learn the new lesson could be more momentous both in time and eternity than physical relief. We are not discounting the value of relief, but we may someday discover that we have concentrated too exclusively on physical relief and too little on spiritual growth. *The Book of Job teaches that it is God's will for us to have both.* Perhaps more people would be healed if they were convinced that their affliction is intended to drive them to God and if they became more interested in knowing Him better.

## GOD'S BENEVOLENT PURPOSE: GROWTH IN HOLINESS

*To allow an affliction to drive one to God, even before the healing comes, may be of more consequence than to receive a healing without the closer relationship with God.* In his book *Guilt and Redemption* Lewis J. Sherrill says, "The bottom of men's hell is a malignant relationship with God. In that breeding ground his other poisons spawn and from it they spread." *If this is true, then nothing is more important than a closer walk with God.* In all God's dealing with us, He is working toward greater holiness, which is only a deeper degree of *agape* love. Let no one deceive you. Whether God does miraculous deliverances or permits sore affliction, all is for one purpose and that is holiness. Be not deceived: *There is nothing greater. There is no social problem that a greater degree of* agape *love will not solve. It will resolve all the stresses and strains of interpersonal relationships whether in the home, church, or state. That is why* agape *love is the essence of holiness.*

## IMPATIENCE WITH GOD

It may be fitting here to quote from a paraphrase of Emmet Fox: "There is no difficulty that enough *agape* love will not conquer; no disease that enough *agape* love will not heal; no door that enough *agape* love will not open; no gulf that enough *agape* love will not bridge; no wall that enough *agape* love will not throw down; no sin that enough *agape* love will not redeem . . . .

"It makes no difference how deeply seated may be the trouble; how hopeless the outlook; how muddled the tangle; how great the mistake. A sufficient realization of *agape* love will disolve it all . . . . If only you could love enough you would be the happiest and most powerful being in the world . . . ."

## LEARNING *AGAPE* LOVE REQUIRES TIME

*God's purpose in permitting adversity is growth in holiness, in* agape *love, and that is obtained by progressive overcoming of the effects of the fall.* This may be more important in God's sight than immediate healing. It is easy enough to say that if a seeker were fully submitted in the beginning, he could be healed without delay, but such is the effect of the fall on the moral nature that yielding and adjustment may not always be easy. The effects of the fall are so ingrained and all pervasive, that sometimes only a supernaturally brilliant revelation from God can expose it. Only in the radiance of the vision of God, high and lifted up, was Isaiah able to see hitherto unrevealed consequences of the fall and when he did, he cried, "Woe is me." Afer a similar vision, Job cried, "I abhor myself." Both of these men were, presumably, advanced in grace. But to uncover hidden traces and stains of their fallen condition required a new revelation. And in Job's case, that revelation came only after a long period of waiting upon God. "And so to me have been allotted months of frustration, these long and weary nights" (Job 7:3, *The Living Bible)*. Because of the fall, discovery and response to God's refining may require time. In Job's case it seemed to be that way. The lesson here is that God has something to say in our afflictions and the essential thing is to get quiet enough to hear God's voice. Because of the results of the fall, combined with Satan's opposition, that may be somewhat of a slow process. *Someone has said that one of the severest tests of character is the ability to wait upon God without losing patience with Him.*

THE RESIDUAL EFFECTS OF THE FALL

*One reason why healing is sometimes postponed could be our failure to more readily overcome the effects of the fall.* Overcoming those effects is what is known as growth in grace. The fall has so disturbed, distorted, and damaged the moral nature that spiritual growth and maturity are greatly impeded, thus hindering faith for healing. The fall has left us maimed, crippled, disoriented, and disorganized in every part of our being. Growth in grace after sanctification and the filling with the Spirit is accomplished by overcoming the residual effects of the fall.

## HEALING DELAYED BY SPIRITUAL RETARDATION

Sometimes faith for healing seems to be given instantaneously. This is especially true of young converts and those without much wrong theology to unlearn. In other cases, growth in faith may be more protracted. Because God is sovereign, many situations defy analysis. It is often a mystery why healing is deferred, especially to the one who is ill. It is easy to lose patience with God and wonder why healing does not always come immediately. However, because the atonement is full and complete, because God's part is already done, *when healing is delayed the trouble must always be on the human side. This is one of the weighty messages in the Book of Job.* If every affliction comes with a message from the heart of God, it is the fallen nature that prevents or hinders our hearing and accepting the new revelation and making the adjustment and receiving faith for healing. *What appears as the slowness of God's method is actually our spiritual dullness, our inability to receive the new light and walk in it.*

## DISILLUSIONMENT WITH SELF

When an affliction strikes, most of us are as utterly unconscious of any fault, failure, or shortcoming as was Job. Because we are totally unconscious of the spiritual imperfection which God sees and from which He is moving to free us, we are constrained to believe that this particular affliction is wholly without meaning. *Many of us are so full of unconscious spiritual pride, complacency, and conceit (the result of the fall) that only adversity can disillusion us with ourselves.* We may discover that this was Job's problem and that it could be ours. Although God testified that Job was a perfect man, his perfection was not absolute. However nearly perfect he may have been, Job was not healed until he was completely disillusioned with himself. And this proved to be a slow process, all because Job, like others of us, was maimed by the fall. *God is compelled to work slowly with us because we could not bear the full revelation of the depth of depravity in our fallen nature even after grace has done its utmost.* We are tempted to lose patience with God because of the protracted and sometimes the seemingly interminable period of waiting. We may some day find that the slowness of God's dealing with us is because of our inability to more readily accept disillusionment with ourselves.

## CONFESS YOUR FAULTS

James recognized this difficulty when he gave instruction in James 5:16. Writing to believers who presumably were filled with the Spirit, he said, "Confess your faults one to another, and pray for one another, that ye may be healed." *Here James recognizes that physical affliction may be the result of some failure in the life of the believer.* It is almost as difficult for one who is considered a mature Christian to recognize, acknowledge, and confess his mistakes, his sins of ignorance, sins of attitude and disposition, sins of failure and omission as it is for an unregenerated sinner to confess his outbroken transgressions. To be saved, sanctified, filled with the Spirit is a marvelous state of grace, but even after the sin nature is cleansed, one is still a fallen human being.

## MAGNITUDE OF THE HUMAN SPIRIT

*The human spirit is the most magnificent and sublime entity in the entire universe next to the Godhead.* It outranks angels, archangels and all other principalities and powers except God Himself. Vast areas of the human personality need to be brought under the sway of the divine Spirit, even *after the works of grace. God is not satisfied merely with our being saved, sanctified or filled with the Spirit.* He is working toward maturity, holiness, the progressive removal of the effects of the fall. All the fall's residue must be considered as corruption because anything less than absolute purity, the purity we will receive in glorification, must be classified as corruption. All of the soulish emotions, the animus or ferment of the flesh, all of the life of nature and of self, all that belongs to the fallen disposition such as impatience, jealousy, resentment, unforgiveness, pride, egoism, spiritual dullness, and insensibility *in any form or degree, conscious or unconscious*—all of this God purposes to refine from our lives, if necessary, by the discipline of affliction. *We may never be made conscious of these defects without suffering, without pain.* Until Job suffered long and deeply he did not become sufficiently disillusioned with himself to receive the new vision of God that revealed to him the corruption of his being, the unrealized dregs of the fall, of which he was previously totally unaware. When he finally received it, the revelation was so shocking that Job, the evangelically perfect, Spirit-filled man, cried out, "I abhor myself and repent in dust and ashes.'' What a surprise this discovery of his uncleanness must have been!

## JOB'S SELF-RIGHTEOUSNESS

The record discloses that Job was not a sinner in the usual sense. He was an upright man, just and righteous by comparative standards, but still suffering from the unrealized devastation of the fall. Through Job God is saying to us, ''I have yet many things to say unto you but you cannot bear them now'' (John 16:12). *He is also saying that even after salvation, sanctification or filling with the Spirit, there is much more refining to be done.* Because the full revelation of the consequences of the fall would probably completely overwhelm us, God is forced to go slowly. As with Job, when God sees we are better prepared and more nearly ready, He opens our eyes, gives us a new vision of Himself and lets us see our own deficiency. Then, as we repent, as Job did, faith for healing becomes possible. *Before Job was healed there was an adjustment to be made. Job had to repent,* apparently not for gross or outbroken sin. It evidently was a residual damage of the fall in matters of attitude and disposition, such as self-complacency, self-vindication and self-defense, some of which are disclosed in his arguments with his comforters.

He was so sure that he was innocent of any wrongdoing that he fluctuated between declaring his own innocence and God's apparent injustice in His providential and governmental dealing with both men and nations. Time after time he pleads his innocence. In chapter 6:29 in answer to Eliphaz, he says, ''Stop assuming my guilt for I am righteous.'' In chapter 10:4-7 he implies that God is unjust: ''Are you (God) unjust like men?'' He accuses God of hounding him for sins which God knows full well Job has not committed. In chapter 12:4 he declares he is a righteous man and in verse 6 he calumniates God's providence when he says that ''robbers prosper even though they provoke God.'' In 13:18 he says, ''I know that I am righteous.'' But in 21:7, ''The truth is that the wicked live on to a good old age and become great and powerful.'' In 21:16, ''Everything the wicked touch has turned to gold.'' But in 23:12 he says, ''I have not refused his commandments but have enjoyed them more than my daily food.'' And in 27:5, 6, ''Until I die I will vow my innocence. I am not a sinner—I repeat it again and again, my conscience is clear for as long as I live'' *(The Living Bible).*

## REASON FOR GOD'S DELAYS

This is a mystery until we remember that if ''sentence against an evil work were executed speedily'' there would be no chance for a voluntary surrender and freedom of a choice in morals and conduct. ''Because sentence against an evil work is not executed speedily, therefore the heart of the sons of men is fully set in them to do evil'' (Ecclesiastes 8:11). If every sinner were cut off immediately at the moment of sin, there would be no opportunity for freedom of moral choice. *There could be no moral universe under any other system than the present one.* Job was mystified and many of us are also mystified because the ''wicked live to a good old age and become great and powerful.'' *But God wants voluntary, not coerced love. Love that is coerced by immediate penalty for transgression is not love at all, as everyone well knows.* For the same reason there could be no moral universe if holiness and righteousness were instantly rewarded. Love that is given because of instantaneous reward would not be true love, that is, *agape* love. It would only be a self-centered love, which is a misnomer.

## GOD WILLING TO BE MISUNDERSTOOD

*We shall see that Job's friends were advocating a universe governed by satanic ethical ideals and principles.* This is a very subtle distinction, but it may explain why a healing is withheld as in Job's case. In fact, it may explain many other divine delays. Job was distressed, as some of us have been, because the wicked live on to a good old age and prosper, even while the righteous suffer. *There can be no testing of character without delays.* During God's delayed reaction to good or evil, God is giving opportunity for self-judgment and self-classification. *By delay, both the righteous and the wicked are given time to make decisions on a moral basis, rather than on the basis of instant reward or punishment.* It gives occasion for the motivation of love and hatred for God to be clarified and developed. By this means, during delay, God is testing and developing character. It is easy to be impatient with God when we fail to understand the purpose of His delay. However, *God is willing to be misunderstood in the universe He has made, in order to achieve His purpose of character development.*

## UNCONSCIOUS SHORTCOMINGS

The passages above indicate that Job was totally unconscious of any shortcoming and that he was sorely tempted to sit in judgment upon God. Job's comforters were convinced otherwise. They believed some hidden sin caused his sickness. In chapter 19 he says, "Ten times now you have declared that I am a sinner." Because Job's affliction was so horrible and revolting, they accused him of brazen, flagrant, heinous violation of God's laws. *This agrees with some theologians who teach that if a believer is not healed immediately it is because he is consciously harboring some secret sin.* We agree that all sickness is the result of man's fallen condition and much sickness is the result of personal transgression. But we know in Job's case it was not overt trespass. Although God used Job as an example both to Satan and the world, God also further refined Job's character. Although Job was totally unconscious of any fault, God worked in him some new revelation of Himself and some new wealth and beauty of character. *And He could do it in no other way in Job and sometimes He can do it no other way in us.*

## RESIDUAL TRAITS OF THE FALLEN NATURE

When grace has achieved its ultimate in overcoming residual traits of the fall in the negatives of evil tempers, jealousies, resentments, harshness, impetuosity, etc., there is an extensive area of positive heavenly virtues, including all the graces of the Spirit, which the fall has either entirely destroyed or severely limited. *Not everyone believes this, but I am convinced there are vast new beauties of God-like character which can never be developed without the discipline of suffering.* Who can love as Jesus loved? Who is willing to die for those who hate him? Who has the infinite compassion of God? Who can forgive as He? Who always prefers others before himself? The totality of God's love is infinite. Because we are fallen creatures the distance between human and divine compassion is immeasurable. Until we have begun to approach more nearly the love and compassion of God, which embraces all mankind, good or evil, there may be need for the discipline of sorrow and suffering in our lives to work that compassion in us.

## SUFFERING WORTH WHAT IT COSTS

*It has been said that there is no love without suffering.* While He is the infinitely joyful God He is also infinite in His vicarious suffering. If you think that the world's sin, vice, degradation, suffering, and sorrow cause you pain, what of the continual anguish of God, Who is all-knowing and all-seeing? "The eyes of the Lord are in every place, beholding the evil and the good" (Proverbs 15:3). *God is vividly conscious of the anguish and pain of all generations of His world—in every clime and nation from creation to the present throbbing moment.* Think of this and then complain of the tribulation, grief, and pain God uses in your life to work in you a more God-like dimension of *agape* love. "Beloved, if God so loved us, we ought also to love one another" (1 John 4:11). *The reasoning is that if an infinitely holy God loved such infinitely less holy people, those infinitely less holy people should be able to love their comparably less holy peers. If those comparably unholy peers are of such value to God because they were created in God's own image they must have intrinsic value and therefore must have worth to those who love God.* "Everyone who loves the Father loves his child as well" (1 John 5:1, NIV). Because deep dimensions of this kind of love develop only in the school of suffering, God may permit it for this reason.

### FRAGMENTATION OF THE BODY OF BELIEVERS

There is another matter that breaks God's heart and that is the fragmentation of His body. If you feel sorrow and pain because of the wounds in Christ's body, if you weep because of the running sores which leave it fractured and broken, dare you drown in self-pity because of the light affliction which He permits in order to generate the love which binds up and heals those running wounds? After grace has done its utmost to discipline us and cleanse us from the negative traits of the fall, there remain infinite dimensions of growth in the positive virtues and graces of the Spirit, *and believe it or not, those graces and virtues will never be developed without suffering.*

### HEALING OF THE SPIRIT

Suppose Job was as nearly perfect as he is pictured. As mature and advanced as he was in the heavenly graces, he still had to explore and appropriate infinite reaches of divine beauty before approximating the infinite compassion of a holy God. How much more may God be seeking to work in us by the mystery, sorrow, tribulation, and pain He permits in our lives. Therefore, the important thing is not primarily to escape the pain, but to accept the new revelation of God and take the new steps in growth that will facilitate faith for healing. Can you accept this? *Healing of the Spirit may be a stepping-stone to healing of the body.* Please don't overlook this possibility.

One of the evidences of God's greatness is that we cannot fathom God's ways with us in an hour or two. One of the evidences of our smallness is that we become discouraged when we cannot understand His providences. It is part of God's greatness and also a tribute to the potential greatness of the human soul that God's dealings with us require time.

## PRINCIPAL LESSONS OF JOB

These, then, are the principal lessons of Job:

1. That all adversity is the result of original sin, but not necessarily of the specific sin of the sufferer.
2. That Satan himself is under God's control. He is not an independent personality or celebrity. He cannot touch one of God's children without God's permission (Job 1:12; 2:6).
3. That Satan causes all adversity, but all adversity, including physical illness, is intended by God to be educational, not necessarily punitive.
4. Every affliction comes with a message from the heart of God.
5. That because we are fallen beings, the delay in healing is not God's but man's fault.
6. That the important thing in every affliction is to receive the new revelation of God and learn the new spiritual lesson.
7. That God's purpose in every affliction is benevolent, intended to prepare us to accept twice as much as we had before and to promote us to higher and more sublime rank both here and hereafter.

In conclusion to this introduction to the Book of Job, we learn from Job's comforters that it is not wise to be too "pat" in our interpretation of God's providences, either with ourselves or with others. If we could fully explain all of God's dealings with us as individuals, we would be as wise as He. If we could take all of the mystery out of life, we would be equal with God in understanding. This should teach us that judgmentalism of other believers is taboo in God's book, as implied in several New Testament passages (Luke 7:37; John 4:11; Romans 14:14).

BASIS OF THIS THEOLOGY

This theology is not based upon the experience of any contemporary individual, but upon the inspired record of God's dealing with Job, who God said was a perfect man. It has survived the test of centuries. I recommend it to you. *Until you have learned to face, overcome, and utilize adversity, you are dangerously vulnerable.* "For we must through *much* tribulation enter into the kingdom of God" (Acts 14:22). As we look at Job we see that the end result is twice as much as before. God is saying through this book that every adversity will pay double your money back when you learn to say with Job, "Though he slay me yet will I trust him" (Job 13:15). This is the only correct reaction to the providences of God and the mysteries of life.

TWO

# MATURITY THROUGH ADVERSITY

## IS AFFLICTION SOMETIMES GOOD?

Most of us have little trouble comprehending why sinners should be under the hand of affliction, but we find it difficult to explain why saints, and especially we ourselves, are so often afflicted. David said, "Before I was afflicted I went astray: but now I have kept thy word . . . . It is good for me that I have been afflicted; that I might learn thy statutes" (Psalm 119:67, 71). David finally became a saint. We readily agree that sickness is not the will of God because it will eventually be banished from God's universe, and that the Lord Jesus has made perfect provision in the atonement for our physical well-being. *And yet here is a Scripture that tells us affliction is sometimes good.*

## SUFFERING: A TOOL FOR REFINEMENT

Some teachers indicate that all the suffering of the believer is the result of his living below God's best plan. We do not believe in suffering for suffering's sake and we do not believe that God does, either. The Word tells us plainly: "He doth not afflict willingly nor grieve the children of men" (Lamentations 3:33). But because of the effect and the damage of the fall to our natures it seems that some suffering, and sometimes much suffering, is necessary for our refinement. Although it is indeed true that Jesus bore our sicknesses and carried our pains, still it seems that because of the disastrous effects of the fall, God cannot create advanced sainthood without suffering and pain. We dare not exclude the necessity at times of physical suffering and pain. If God sees that the only way He can work out in your life and mine the beautiful pattern which He has in mind is by permitting an affliction, who are we to say to Him, "Nay"?

## CHILD TRAINING

As parents it is not our will to cause any of our children pain. But in order to attain the higher end of character training, sometimes it seems needful. Any fond parent would much prefer to take upon himself, in his own body, the pain which he inflicts upon his child in chastisement. And there is a very real sense in which a godly parent does suffer with his child. But to accomplish the higher purpose of character training, he cannot take the suffering upon himself and spare the child. He must permit the suffering, which he would gladly bear, and which in fact God did bear for every one of His children. He must permit that suffering and pain actually to fall upon the child. *A truly wise parent knows that it would be a cruel kindness to his child to shield him and refuse to allow him to suffer when he needs correction.* When we speak about the correction of a child of God we are not thinking primarily of the practice of overt, outbroken sin. We are concerned rather with the refining and purifying of disposition, character, motives, ideals, and purposes. We have in mind the overcoming of the residual consequences of the fall which remain after the experiences of grace.

## NO DEPTH OF SAINTHOOD WITHOUT SUFFERING

When any person deliberately chooses God's best with any depth of purpose, God may take him through a course of child training that may involve suffering, even physical suffering. Could we deny God the privilege and right to use the rod of physical pain if He sees it is the best way to produce His purpose in an individual's life? *It is doubtful that anyone reaches truly great sainthood without suffering, and at times the greatest saints have been the greatest sufferers.*

## A DEEPER BREAKING

Let us take a look at Job as an illustration. Don't forget that he was the outstanding saint of his day, *possibly of all time.* Although he was an Old Testament saint he had all the earmarks of a New Testament Spirit-filled believer. Job doubtless had already suffered before the time when the biblical narrative begins. He had certainly gone through much breaking already, because God said he was perfect, that is, *in a relative sense.* A partially matured apple may be as perfect for its stage of development as a fully ripe one. In this sense Job was a perfect man, but his spiritual development was incomplete. *God saw that he needed a deeper breaking.* Evidently God saw something in Job that needed a greater discipline. I am not saying anything now about God's purpose to use Job as an example for the sake of the sick and suffering down through the ages, but there was evidently something that God saw in Job that needed further maturing. *For one thing, it seems he needed to be broken regarding material possessions.* No one is prepared for God's highest service until he is broken concerning earth and its fading sweets.

## MATERIALISM AND SPIRITUAL AUTHORITY

*The desire for wealth, affluence, the emoluments of fame and fortune is fatal to real sainthood and spiritual authority. According to Jesus, love of mammon cannot co-exist with love for God* (Matthew 6:24). John tells us that pride of possessions is not of the Father, but is of the world (1 John 2:15). Because covetousness is a symptom of the fall and of Satan's syndrome, *it disqualifies anyone from exercising authority in the realm of alien spirits. No one is qualified to wield that power who has not been broken concerning materialism.* He may build an earthly kingdom, and many do, but not an eternal one. Job was an affluent man, a nabob of wealth (Job 1:3). Evidently God, Who knows all hearts, saw that he required a breaking in this area. *More than one man of great spiritual promise has been shipwrecked upon the shoal of covetousness.* Be warned: It is deadly. That is why God warns against it and must keep us dead to it (1 Timothy 6:6-10).

## SELF-CLASSIFICATION

*God's great purpose in setting life in a temporal environment is to teach eternal values and priorities.* God is allowing us to classify ourselves. By our attitude toward material things we are deciding which is more important, time or eternity, the body or the spirit, things that perish or things that remain. *Life on earth is an apprenticeship in which we are learning eternal values.* We are here for one purpose and one alone. That is to learn eternal principles.

*IF I GAINED THE WORLD BUT LOST THE SAVIOR*

*If I gained the world but lost the Savior,*
*Were my life worth living for a day,*
*Could my yearning soul find rest and comfort*
*In the things that soon must pass away?*

*If I gained the world but lost the Savior,*
*Would my gain be worth the life-long strife,*
*Are all earthly pleasures worth comparing*
*For a moment with a Christ-filled life?*

*Had I wealth and love in fullest measure*
*And a name revered both far and near,*
*Yet no hope beyond, nor harbor waiting*
*Where my storm tossed vessel could be still;*

*If I gained the world but lost the Savior,*
*Who endured the Cross and died for me,*
*Could then all the world afford a refuge*
*Whither in my anguish I might flee?*

*O the joy of having all in Jesus!*
*What a balm the broken heart to heal;*
*Ne'er a sin so great but He'd forgive it,*
*Not a sorrow that He does not heal.*

*If I have but Jesus, only Jesus—*
*Nothing else in all the world beside,*
*O, then everything is mine in Jesus,*
*For I need not more. He will provide.*

Anna Olander

## NO PAMPERED SAINTS

You may disagree on this point and we do not seek to coerce your thinking, but we believe that indulgence of the body, overindulgence of the flesh, militates against the development of spiritual life. Paul said, "I keep under my body" (1 Corinthians 9:27). *There never was a great character who did not discipline his body. There is no heroism without material self-denial.* Ralph Waldo Emerson concurs:

*A Hero is not fed on sweets,*
*Daily his own heart he eats;*
*Chambers of the great are jails,*
*And headwinds right for royal sails.*

*I doubt if there ever was a great saint who was not broken in his ambition for worldly possessions and comforts. Self sacrifice is the law of the universe.* Living for self is always counterproductive. Solemnly consider these significant lines:

*Jesus and Alexander died at thirty-three.*
*One lived and died for self; One died for you and me.*
*The Greek died on a throne; the Jew died on a cross;*
*One's life a triumph seemed; the other but a loss.*
*One led vast armies forth; the other walked alone;*
*One shed a whole world's blood; the other gave His own.*
*One won the world in life and lost it all in death;*
*The other lost His life to win the whole world's faith.*

*Jesus and Alexander died at thirty-three,*
*One died in Babylon; and one on Calvary.*

*One gained all for self; and one Himself He gave;*
*One conquered every throne; the other every grave.*
*The one made himself God; the God made Himself less:*
*The one lived but to blast; the other but to bless.*
*When died the Greek, forever fell his throne of swords;*
*But Jesus died to live forever Lord of lords.*

*Jesus and Alexander died at thirty-three,*
*The Greek made all men slaves; the Jew made all men free.*
*One built a throne on blood; the other built on love,*
*The one was born of earth; the other from above;*
*One won all this earth, to lose all earth and heaven;*
*The other gave up all, that all to Him might be given.*
*The Greek forever died; the Jew forever lives.*
*He loses all who gets, and wins all things who gives.*

Author unknown

CROWNS CAST IN CRUCIBLES

That is the lesson of the cross. *Tribulation's imprint is on all great saints. It has been said that crowns are cast in crucibles, and chains of character that wind about the feet of God are forged in earthly flames.* No man is greatest victor until he has trodden the winepress of woe. With seams of anguish deep in his brow, the Man of sorrows said, "In the world you shall have tribulation" (John 16:33). *Blood marks the steps that lead to the heights.*

GRIEF AND GREATNESS

It has been well said, *"Our crowns will be wrested from the giants we conquer. Grief has always been the lot of greatness."* It is an open secret that *"the mark of rank in nature is capacity for pain, and the anguish of the singer makes the sweetness of the strain."* Most of us feel that as soon as we give ourselves to God in full consecration, things ought to run smoothly, but God cannot make us until He first "breaks" us. He cannot mold us until He melts us. He cannot melt us except by fire.

ILL-CLAD AND KNOCKED ABOUT

God has indeed promised to supply all of our needs, but the very man who wrote this Scripture, "My God shall supply all your needs," also said in 1 Corinthians 4:11, 12, "To this very hour we both hunger and thirst, we are ill-clad and knocked about. We work hard for our living" *(Phillips)*. I do not know how Paul would reconcile that statement with his wonderful promise in Philippians 4:19, "My God shall supply all your needs, according to his riches in glory by Christ Jesus." There is never any lack in any life because of a short supply in heaven's storehouse or because of God's indifference. *The reason is always on the human side.* But Paul evidently recognized that if God was to keep alive in his life that heroic spirit of self-sacrifice, he must occasionally permit him to experience need.

In the 4th chapter of Philippians, before Paul wrote this wonderful promise, he said, "How grateful I am and how I praise the Lord that you are helping me again. I know you have always been anxious to send what you could, but for awhile you didn't have the chance. Not that I was ever in need, for I have learned how to get along happily whether I have much or little. I know how to live on almost nothing or with everything. I have learned the secret of contentment in every situation, whether it be a full stomach or hunger, plenty or want; for I can do everything God asks me to with the help of Christ who gives me the strength and power'' *(The Living Bible).*

NOTHING INTRINSICALLY EVIL

It is no great accomplishment to be victorious in prosperity. Almost anyone can shine then. The real problem is how to live triumphantly in privations. Paul had them and most of us have them. *Until you have learned to face, overcome and utilize adversity, you are dangerously vulnerable,* because Paul tells us in Acts 14:22 that ''we must through much tribulation enter into the kingdom of God.'' We cannot avoid tribulation, adversity, and affliction, but if we understand that these things may be good, *that nothing intrinsically evil can come to a child of God, that only a wrong reaction can injure him; if he learns how to utilize his problems for spiritual growth, then he has it made. If God's blessings are our good and if Satan's assaults are transformed into blessings by our reaction, we have nothing to fear because everything is working for our good.*

THE BEST POSSIBLE UNIVERSE

It is a comfort to know that if God is God, the universe He has made is the best one possible. This is what Browning meant when he said,

> *''God's in His heaven*
> *All's right with the world.''*

This does not mean that there is no evil in God's universe. *It does mean that God is using that evil for His purpose. His purpose is to obtain and train an eternal companion for His Son who is to rule and reign with Him in the ages to come.* That companion can never be trained in overcoming without an antagonist. God could have eliminated Satan at his fall, but He is using him in the selection, training, and development of His eternal companion. He could do it in no other kind of universe than one exactly like this one. If this universe were not the best universe possible, then God would not be God, that is, He would not be supreme.

*WATCH GOD'S METHODS*

*When God wants to drill a man,*
*And thrill a man*
*And skill a man,*
*When God wants to mold a man*
*To play the noblest part;*
*When He yearns with all His heart*
*To create so great and bold a man*
*That all the world shall be amazed,*
*Watch His methods, watch His ways!*
*How He ruthlessly perfects*
*Whom He royally elects:*
*How He hammers him and hurts him,*
*And with mighty blows converts him*
*Into trial shapes of clay which*
*Only God understands;*
*While his tortured heart is crying*
*And he lifts beseeching hands!*
*How he bends but never breaks*
*When his good He undertakes;*

*How with every purpose fuses him;*
*By every act induces him*
*To try his splendor out—*
*God knows what He's about.*

Dale Martin Stone

NOT A HOLIDAY TASK

*It is dubious if anyone is qualified for God's highest service until he is broken concerning material things.* Material things are necessary, but they can easily overabsorb one. Overwhelming occupation with material things may disqualify one from successful promotion of things that are eternal. If one is too occupied with temporal things he cannot orient or direct others toward the eternal. *If he is not delivered from love of earth himself, he cannot deliver anyone else.* This is why God cannot use for high spiritual service those who have not been broken concerning wealth and affluence. This is why Paul exhorts the Colossians to "Set your affections on things above, not on things on the earth" (Colossians 3:2). Maclaren says: "There is a true asceticism, a 'gymnastic unto godliness' as Paul calls it. Without rigid self-control and self-limitation, there is no vigorous faith and no effective work." *It is no holiday task to cast out devils. Self-indulgent men will never do it.* Loose-braced, easygoing souls that lie open to all the pleasurable influences of ordinary life are not fit for God's weapons.

BROKEN REGARDING EARTHLY POSSESSIONS

*Beloved, when God wanted to make a great saint out of Job, He began by breaking him regarding his earthly possessions and comforts.* Likewise, before God can safely entrust anyone with a large ministry he should be dead to earth and its fading sweets. We are living in a day when religion has become big business, so much so that it has attracted the attention of the news media as represented by metropolitan newspapers, national magazines, and nationwide television. *When large sums become available for God's work, there is grave danger of careless stewardship.* The money given is God's money and He will hold us accountable at the judgment for unconscientious use of it. That money, released by the supernatural operation of God's Spirit, through fasting and prayer, represents God's interest in souls. *He will hold us responsible for the souls that are lost because of careless use of consecrated treasure.*

PROSPERITY VERSUS ABSTEMIOUS LIVING

When large sums of wealth are given for spiritual purposes, unless one is truly broken regarding material things, the temptation is great to play fast and loose with money. *For this reason every child of God should live as frugally as is consistent with efficiency.* Not many of us can say, as a friend of mine recently said, "The more generous my income, the more frugal my life style." In a world where more than 100,000 souls a day are passing to Christless graves, *it ill becomes any child of God to be self-indulgent.* Not everyone will accept this, but in a social order where millions have never even heard the name of Jesus, it is inconsistent, to say the least, for any child of God to live any other way except *abstemiously.* When hundreds of millions perish daily without the Bread of Life, how can "the soul in us longer live" if we indulge in needless luxury? *In a world like this, no spiritual leader should live in ostentatious affluence, the gospel of prosperity notwithstanding.* Even though the Word supports the gospel of prosperity, that is only one side of the coin. No man is prepared for the most effective service to God until he is broken concerning material possessions, because no man can serve both God and money (Matthew 6:24).

## MANAGERS, NOT OWNERS

This is true, not only of pastors and evangelists, but of every layman as well. There is a temptation to feel that since you earned your fortune by your own ingenuity, talent, or business acumen, it is yours to use as you please. But God anticipated this in Deuteronomy 8:17-18: "You may say to yourself, 'My power and the strength of my hands have produced this wealth for me.' But remember the Lord your God, for it is he who gives you the ability to produce wealth" (NIV). You could not move an eyelash without Him. You owe Him the very breath you breathe. *You are only a steward.* Not only one-tenth of your income belongs to Him, but everything to which you lay claim. *You are only a manager.* "What? Know ye not that . . .ye are not your own? For ye are bought with a price: therefore glorify God in your body, and in your spirit, which are God's" (1 Corinthians 6:19, 20). *God had to break Job regarding earthly possessions because no man is properly prepared for God's service until he is broken concerning material things.*

## TWO SIDES OF A COIN

The story of Job raises the question, "Why do good people seem to suffer sometimes more than others?"

Why are the best people at times placed in such trying, difficult, strenuous, painful, and mysterious circumstances? Cannot God keep His Word? How does it come that we are ever put in a difficult situation, physically or financially, when God said that He would supply *all* of our needs according to His riches in glory? Is He failing to keep His Covenant? How is it that some people who believe and teach divine healing, for instance, on some occasions seem unable to take healing in their present need? Why is it that those who have been healed at one time cannot seemingly manifest healing at another? *Not everyone will concede this, but because of our fallen condition, God cannot always make us strong without the discipline of pain.*

This does not mean that God has not borne our pain and carried our sorrows, but rather that if we are to be strong He cannot always shield us from adversity. Someone has said, "God never wastes His children's pain. God loves much those whom He trusts with sorrow, and designs some precious soul enrichment which comes only through the shadow of suffering. *There are things which even God cannot do for us unless He allows us to suffer.*" Divine truth is never contradictory, but like a coin it has two sides.

## AN ETERNAL HERITAGE

Health—spiritual, physical, mental, and material—is the eternal heritage of every born-again child of God and is available here and now in proportion to its spiritual importance. Health in all of these areas is provided in the atonement which originated before the foundation of the world. Calvary is an eternal fact in the heart of God. But if

God sees that the only way He can get one to heaven or to mature him spiritually is by affliction, then thank Him for it. "Before I was afflicted, I went astray, but now have I kept thy word," said David in Psalm 119:67, and he is not the only one who has been brought back to God by affliction. The writer of Psalm 107 testified also concerning this point: "Fools because of their transgression, and because of their iniquities, are afflicted. Their soul abhors all manner of meat; and they draw near unto the gates of death. Then they cry unto the Lord in their trouble, and he saveth them out of their distresses. He sent his word and healed them, and delivered them from their destructions" (Psalm 107:17-19). Therefore, it appears that divine healing is always God's will if and when it aids and promotes spiritual growth.

## ALL THINGS ARE YOURS

*Unquestionably, divine life is provided in the atonement* (Isaiah 53). But listen: "There are things which even God cannot do for us unless He allows us to suffer." One cannot have the result of the process without the process. If you are among those that love God all things are yours (1 Corinthians 3:21-23). The stars in their courses fight for you. Every wind that blows can only fill your sails. God does not test worthless souls. There is something good in you, beloved, if God is testing you sorely and severely. *Even if there is an easy way to get to heaven, I am not sure I would be comfortable there without any battle scars.* How about you? The writer of these lines apparently feels the same way:

*Hast thou no scar?*<br>
*No hidden scar on foot, or side, or hand?*<br>
*I hear thee sung as mighty in the land.*<br>
*I hear them hail thy bright ascendant star,*<br>
*Hast thou no scar?*<br>
*Hast thou no wound?*<br>
*Yet I was wounded by the archers, spent,*<br>
*Leaned me against a tree to die: and rent*<br>
*By ravening wolves that compassed me, I swooned:*<br>
*Has thou no wound?*<br>
*No wound? No scar?*<br>
*Yet, as the Master shall the servant be,*<br>
*And pierced are the feet that follow Me:*<br>
*But thine are whole: can He have followed far*<br>
*Who hath no wound nor scar?*

Author unknown

Job was a wealthy man. "He was the greatest man of all the people of the East" (Job 1:3). God had blessed him with prestige and prosperity. But God wanted to do something more in Job's life, so He let him be broken where material possessions were concerned. If God is going to entrust any of us with responsibility in His work, He may have to take us also through a discipline by which we are broken regarding earth and its comforts and joys.

# THREE
# THE SEED PLANTED IN MEXICO

## THE BREAKING OF DOMESTIC AFFECTION

Another point upon which Job may have needed breaking was his domestic affections, his family life. You remember that in one day his sons and his daughters were slain, supposedly by a so-called "act of God." And in the midst of all this grief and sorrow he did not charge God foolishly. He did not see the purpose. He did not comprehend why. But he bowed in humble submission. To be broken as to natural affection is a deeper breaking than a financial breaking—plainly Job needed it, and we need it on some occasions, too. Who of us would not gladly see all of his wealth disappear and still feel that he was rich if his loved ones were spared?

Devotion to one's family is admirable, noble, thoroughly Christian; it is a biblical command (Ephesians 5:25, 28, 33; Titus 2:4). In 1 Timothy 5:8 Paul insists, "If anyone does not provide for his relatives and especially for his immediate family, he has denied the faith and is worse than an unbeliever." But it may become overweening. Jesus has told us that it is possible to love them more than the Savior Himself (Matthew 10:37). To correct our priorities, God may take us through a breaking on the point of family love and affection. *Even family life and devotion must be second to love for Christ.* Jesus said, ''If any man come after me and hate not his father and mother and wife and children, brethren and sisters, yea, and his own life also, he cannot be my disciple'' (Luke 14:26). If we are Christ's slaves, then all that we possess belongs to Him. He can do anything which He pleases, not only with us, but with our loved ones as well. Before Christ can be our all and in all, God may have to break us in respect to natural affection. This love, high and holy as it is, still must rank second to love for the Lord Jesus Christ. When we enter a special covenant, a blood covenant between our soul and our Lord, He must always be first. *And He may test us on this point to see whether our spiritual devotion comes only from our teeth out, or whether we really mean it. There may be something that God cannot accomplish in us without giving permission to Satan to lay his hand upon those who are dear to us.* Love must be ready to lay them upon the altar either of sacrifice or service, and even death.

This matter of domestic affection is a sensitive area. Like some of us, Job may have needed a greater maturity regarding his children. Even the best of men do now and then. Although the Word says Job was perfect, his perfection was relative rather than ultimate or absolute. Possibly his family was less mature than he. The fact that following their birthday parties he felt it imperative to ''sanctify'' them indicates there may have been breaches of piety, requiring repentance and restitution.

This may not be too surprising, even in preachers' families. Not all of us always set the best example in the church and community. Not every minister has been as wise as godly parents should be. And a number have, at least temporarily, lost their children to the world. Satan obviously concentrates upon the undoing, ruination, and wrecking of the preacher's family circle above most others. It is one of his highest priorities.

## A BETTER APPROACH

In recent years, some pastors have advocated a better approach to the family problem. They have adopted the following formula: God first, family second, and profession third. I never heard of this in my earlier years. I know now that, like some others, I made some mistakes, the same mistakes that many pastors still make. I thought that God's work, considered from an organizational standpoint, should have first consideration. I thought that the only way God could be first was by putting His work first. This is a delicate question. Some spiritual leaders have found the biblical balance and have saved their families.

For those who have thus far failed with their families, what is the best, the biblical approach? Is there no hope for them? Must they succumb to defeat? By no means. God has provided a plan. It begins in brokenness and repentance. Where we have sinned, blundered, and fallen short, the immediate thing is to acknowledge error, take full responsibility for it and, as far as possible, make restitution.

The devil wants all of us to think there is no way to recover, no way to overcome the mistakes of the past. He is a liar and the father of lies. Every parent who is truly contrite may be certain of the help of Almighty God. There are two passages of Scripture specifically for the parent whom Satan has deceived with the lie that he has permanently "blown it" with his family. One is Isaiah 54:13: "And all thy children (descendants) shall be taught of the Lord, and great shall be the peace (prosperity) of thy children." Another is Isaiah 49:25: "For I will contend with him that contendeth with thee, and I will save thy children." If you doubt that you have the right to stand upon this Word, turn to 2 Corinthians 1:20: "For all the promises of God in him are yea and in him Amen, unto the glory of God by us." This is the guarantee that in Christ Jesus all the redemption promises that have ever been spoken by the mouth of God are confirmed and available to every believer now. If you appropriate these promises and never give up, God is bound by His Word to bring your child to Himself regardless of his present condition.

This disproves Satan's propaganda that it is no longer of any use for parents to pray for the salvation of a rebellious child. Too long have we endured Satan's argument that God will not coerce a person's will. That is true. He will not. But God has given the Church authority over all the power of the enemy (Luke 10:19) and if you will persevere, if you will not surrender your child to Satan, God is honor bound by His Word to find a means, not to coerce, but to persuade him to repent, change his mind, and yield to the all-availing love of the Lord Jesus Christ. If the child will not come without chastisement, God will take care of that. If you do not give in to satanic deceptions and bluff, God will so convict your child that he will find it easier to submit than to continue his rebellion.

Satan is not supreme in the universe. God has

the power to overcome rebellion in your child. The key is not primarily the Satan-inspired state of mind of your child, but your own dedication and determination. You are the key because prayer is on the job training. In 1 John 5:14 the Word is clear: "And this is the confidence that we have in him, that, if we ask anything according to his will, he heareth us; and if we know that he hear us, whatsoever we ask, we know that we have the petitions that we desired of him."

Parents of rebellious children are not helpless. If they will never give up the fight, they do not have to be defeated. We shall learn later that Job found the right course and saved his family. Not all of my descendants are safely in the fold yet, but I believe they will be. I believe that in answer to prayer, God will continue to pursue them by His Spirit, until, like their ancestor, they find it easier to surrender than to continue in their resistance.

## OUR CORN OF WHEAT

In 1942 I felt compelled to take a missionary trip. I use the term "compel" advisedly because the sense of urgency was so powerful that I felt I would burn up inside if I failed to heed the call. Our firstborn, Paul Rollin, had graduated from high school the previous spring and was considering entering Moody Bible Institute. The possibility of a missionary trip captured his imagination and when friends in our radio audience provided the means for his transportation, he eagerly accepted.

Because World War II had interfered with overseas travel, the only mission field available at that time was Latin America. Since Paul Rollin was approaching eighteen and subject to military draft, the government approved his visa to travel only so far as Mexico.

The Oriental Missionary Society had decided to open work in South America and was sending veteran missionaries Roy Adams and Charles Culver to explore and select a location. Both Mrs. Billheimer and Paul Rollin joined Brother Culver and me from Anderson to Mexico City, where we met Brother Adams. Together we spent some time visiting various missions in Mexico. Before the schedule led us further, our small son, David Robb, developed serious illness and Mrs. Billheimer had to fly home, leaving Paul Rollin in Mexico with a mission that worked among the mountain Indians.

In the month following our parting, Paul Rollin worked among them under the direction of the mission. He not only became fascinated with them, but fell in love with the work and testified that God was calling him to help reach the unreached Indians of the mountains.

During the Easter season in early April, I had arrived in Colombia where I was visiting a mission school in the town of Cali. While I was there, the head of the mission showed me a family photograph containing the picture of his oldest son, who had recently returned to Canada to pursue his education. He had suddenly been taken ill and had died. My heart bled for the father as he told the story. Little did I suspect that on the morning after Easter, about the time I was boarding the train to leave Cali, my own son would be losing his life in the Valles River in Mexico, and that Mrs. Billheimer would have to make the decision alone for his burial. Because I was in transit to Quito, Ecuador, it was impossible to contact me.

When word of Paul Rollin's accidental drowning reached home, our friends insisted that his mother bring his body home for burial. However, Mrs. Billheimer felt that he should remain among the Indians he had come to love.

Paul Rollin drowned early Monday morning, April 6, 1942, the morning after Easter. I reached Quito the next Wednesday after midnight. As I entered the hotel, the news was given to me. The fact that Mrs. Billheimer and I were so widely separated in that hour made our grief unspeakably more poignant. By that time our son was already interred.

In the tropics burial must follow death quickly. At his funeral the morning following his fatal accident, the head of the mission, Dr. Francisco Soltero, took for his funeral text, John 12:24: "Except a corn of wheat fall into the ground and die, it abideth alone, but if it die, it bringeth forth much fruit." This was the passage which the Spirit quickened to Mrs. Billheimer as she made funeral decisions, and at the same time to me. On my first night in Quito I spoke by shortwave radio to my family and friends in Anderson, Indiana. It was possible for me to speak to them over the facilities of HCJB, the Pioneer Missionary Broadcaster, a radio station heard both then and now around the world. John 12:24 was also the same verse which I used the next Sunday when I spoke through those facilities to the memorial service that was held in our Tabernacle at home. The entire Tabernacle audience was able to hear my message, but I could receive communications from them only by cable.

On my return from the trip, several months later, Mrs. Billheimer and two of our children met me in

Valles, Mexico. Together we followed the course of the funeral procession to the gravesite where, with tears flowing freely, we knelt as a family and thanked God that we had one treasure safe in heaven.

Yet our son's death by drowning on the mission field seemed to us a terrible mistake. He was only eighteen. God had blessed him with unusual talent in gospel music, both vocal and instrumental. At his graduation from high school he had won a scholarship in voice to Indiana University. At that time radio music was almost totally "live." Recording was in its infancy. Although so young, Paul Rollin filled a very large place in our radio music. Because of this he wielded a large influence throughout the radio audience. He could play almost any instrument he chose. He handled organ, piano, and trombone skillfully. His ear was perfect. He was superb in both solo and group performance. During his last two years of high school he carried a major portion of our radio music in two daily programs and several on Sunday. We did not see how we could operate without him.

We have never been the same. We had to return to the microphone without his accomplished voice and musical talent. But in the years that followed, thousands of dollars were poured out in his memory to provide scholarships for a large number of young Indian students who, over the years, have taken his place in the whitened harvest fields. Yes, it seemed a terrible loss to us, but in the decades after his death many young people both in Mexico and the States arose to take his place.

You can do two things with a grain of wheat. It may be eaten or sown. Our grain of wheat is buried in Mexico. The following lines illustrate the truth of this beautiful Scripture passage. They were written by Dr. Paul Updike, now deceased, who was saved and healed of an incurable disease under our ministry and later became a district superintendent in the Church of the Nazarene.

*He walked in the fields of ripened grain*
*and rejoiced for the morning sun;*
*Fresh was his faith for the Gospel gain*
*As a worker just begun.*

*'Twas not a heart halfway given,*
*Waiting till day was done;*
*His was a soul passion-driven*
*To work for the Holy One.*

*'Twas not a hand nerve-wracked, unsteady,*
*That plied the sickle there;*
*His was a firm, strong one.*
*And ready to launch out—and dare.*

*He fell in the field, but not in vain,*
*For he left his sickle there:*
*There lies his faith, and hope for the grain,*
*His love, his heart, and prayer.*

*Others must take up his reaping hook*
*And reap while the day wears on;*
*Then they will share in the harvest book:*
*He fell, but he will still live on.*

Before they were born, each of our children was dedicated to God for either sacrifice or service. Evidently God saw that we needed a deeper breaking. Paul Rollin's early and apparently untimely death was a devastating blow to us. However, in ways beyond our ken, God sustained both Mrs. Billheimer and me. In the succeeding difficult days and months we found great comfort in knowing that many young people at home and abroad had been inspired and challenged to take up the sickle he had laid down and were entering the ripened harvest field. Today, many years later, they continue their fruitful labor.

## AN UNEXPECTED DIVIDEND

Some unanticipated spiritual dividends arose from this sorrow. Shortly after my return, a brother pastor, one of the leading pastors and evangelists of his denomination, called at the Tabernacle. Since he had been openly hostile to our ministry, I was astonished to find him uncontrollably weeping. I was even more astonished when he finally regained sufficient composure to speak. He began by telling me how utterly shaken he had been by watching the way God had sustained us in our loss. Mrs. Billheimer was alone when the blow came and unable to communicate with me, yet she had made the decision by herself to permit Paul Rollin's burial on foreign soil. She had withstood the urging of many to bring his body home for interment. This pastor had listened to Mrs. Billheimer on the local broadcasts as she perisisted in working at the microphone. He had also heard me speak to family and friends by shortwave on the broadcasts from Quito, Ecuador. He himself had a son near Paul Rollin's age. Between sobs he said that if he had been in my place, instead of finishing that tour he would have returned at once.

Suddenly he made a remarkable confession. Although he was one of the leading exponents of Wesley's doctrine of entire sanctification, he had been critical of my emphasis on the progressive work of the Holy Spirit following the crisis. Through sensing the utterness of our submission, he had discovered that he himself was not living in the fullness of the blessing. Then he knelt and asked me to lay hands upon him and pray that he might be filled. That experience transformed him and he was prepared to meet the Lord when a few years later he was stricken with terminal cancer. Through the brokenness God had to work in us, God was able to produce a new brokenness in his life and prepare him for his own homegoing.

God saw that we required the same kind of brokenness as Job. None of us has reached the point where we are truly broken so long as we sit in judgment upon any act of God. Job said, "The Lord gave and the Lord taketh away. Blessed be the name of the Lord" (Job 1:21). He was truly broken in that regard and we are not fully subdued until we have reached that same depth of submission.

FOUR
# THE USES OF PHYSICAL AFFLICTION

## JOB NEEDED TO BE BROKEN PHYSICALLY

God readily saw something in Job which needed the discipline of a period of broken health for "He does not afflict willingly or grieve the children of men" (Lamentations 3:33). It appears that Job needed to be broken not only concerning material things, not only concerning his personal affections, but concerning his physical life as well. Regardless of the gospel of healing, there are areas in the spiritual life which may not be developed without the discipline of physical limitation. In 1 Timothy 4:8 Paul says, "Physical training is of some value, but godliness has value for all things, holding promise for both the present life and the life to come" (NIV). Overoccupation with physical well-being may not always promote spiritual values. There may be some outstanding Christian coaches and athletes and some Christians in professional sports. It may not be impossible to serve Christ in the gymnastic world. In recent years spiritual life has seemed to penetrate certain professional athletic groups. *But outstanding saints in sports are probably the exception rather than the rule.* Overoccupation with the body, overfascination with its exploitation and development may dwarf the spirit. Although the body is eternal, it is incidental to the spirit and its eternal welfare is dependent upon the cultivation of the inner man. *Man has a body but he is a spirit.* The spirit is the real person. To prevent one from overfascination with the physical, to enable one to keep his priorities straight, God may possibly permit one to be broken in health. He did in the case of Job. All affliction is from Satan, but God may at times overrule it for good. "Before I was afflicted, I went astray; but now have I kept thy word" (Psalm 119:67). Many wayward people, many backsliders, including David, have been brought back to God by physical illness.

## A BITTER CUP

I'm not suggesting that nobody is mightily used of God unless he has had physical problems, but many people who have been so employed have passed through the vale of deep bodily suffering beforehand. Although God is not the author of sickness of calamity, yet since He sometimes needs broken people, He permitted Satan to reduce Job lower and lower. Perhaps not everyone has to have this kind of discipline, but in certain situations God may have no other way to achieve His purpose. It was only after more than three years of agonizing sorrow, suffering, and heartache in total disability from deadly tuberculosis that God was able to discipline me into fuller submission. Since then God gave my wife and me more than fifty-five years of rewarding ministry.

## DON'T CHASE A "RED HERRING"

"Therefore, since Christ suffered in his body, arm

yourselves with the same attitude, because he who has suffered in his body is done with sin. As a result, he does not live the rest of his earthly life for evil human desires, but rather for the will of God. For you have spent enough time in the past doing what pagans choose to do—living in debauchery, lust, drunkenness, orgies, carousing and detestable idolatry'' (1 Peter 4:1-3). This indicates that God may use physical affliction and bodily pain to wean one from sinful pleasures and concentrate his attention upon God and the development of the spirit. The body is important; physical well-being is of some value, *but God's primary interest is in the human spirit, which is the real person.* He is sufficiently interested in the heart that He may allow affliction of the body when necessary to focus attention upon spiritual growth. This passage in Peter suggests that affliction may be meaningful, that it may have a purpose and may come with a message. In order to achieve His higher aim of the development and growth of the inner being, God may therefore permit one to be broken in his physical life. If so, the thing of most consequence is not primarily to get rid of the pain, but to hear God's voice, learn the new lesson, and make the spiritual adjustment. If we fail to do this, if we concentrate wholly upon physical relief, that may be counterproductive both physically and spiritually. We believe 100 percent in the ''faith'' message. But faith may be delayed by overoccupation with the body and its comfort and our failure to center on growth of the spirit. *In God's sight, growth in the spirit is paramount.* ''Faith'' teaching which ignores this may be unproductive. If you think that God's primary purpose in providing healing is your physical comfort instead of spiritual growth, you may be chasing a red herring. If sickness is a result of the fall, then progress in overcoming the effects of the fall should place one on the ground or foundation of faith for healing. The experience of Enoch should make this plain.

# FIVE
# NO ACCIDENTS

## BROKEN RELIGIOUSLY

There is another sense in which many have to be broken before God can use them satisfactorily, and that is in regard to religious opinions. This is one of the last and most difficult crushings of all. Most of us, when it comes to our religious notions, have a tendency to set up our particular concepts as little icons and worship them more than God. Our religious ideas, our doctrines, our specific views or convictions on spiritual things all become so dear to us that they have a tendency to crowd God Himself into the background and take His place. This is what occurred between Job and his comforters. And so God may have to break us in this regard.

## DOCTRINE OF HEALING

Take for instance our current ideas about the doctrine of healing. Most of us assume that God has supplied healing in the atonement for the body as well as for the soul. If we are not careful, we will set up our specific convictions on that doctrine as a kind of golden calf and we will seek to groove everyone else along the line of our ideas. If people do not accept our opinions immediately, we discount their spirituality, indicating that we have placed our religious conception as a god instead of God Himself. Maintaining proper balance in these matters requires great care.

### "CRIBBED AND CABINED" VIEWS

Although God said that Job was a perfect man, we see later that Job had some religious ideas that had to go. His brothers are not all dead yet. If we are not careful we will erect our denomination in the place of God, and the views of our separate religious group will set the boundaries of our spiritual comprehension. When this happens we cannot go beyond the vision of our particular sectarian persuasions. *Then we cannot deal directly with God.* Denominationalism has been a blessing. We would make it clear that we are not antidenominational. Denominations have been employed to recover and emphasize formerly neglected truths, but there is a tendency to establish the designated doctrines of our religious movement as "whole truth and nothing but the truth." We become shaped by our denominational views. We become spiritually "cribbed and cabined." When we do that, God may have to break us because our usefulness may be severely limited. God wants us sufficiently yielded so that we do not unduly formulate other people and crowd out the work of the Holy Spirit in them. *We need to recognize that God blesses many people outside of our particular group and spiritual clique.* The brokenness that God wrought in Job He seeks to work in every life that He uses in large degrees. *God broke Job regarding his possessions, regarding his domestic affections, regarding his health, and finally, regarding his religious precepts.*

## SUFFERING AS AN ACCIDENT

One of the differences between Job and his comforters was over the question of the suffering of the righteous. This same question divides people today. To answer it correctly is not essential to salvation. Yet indifferent schools of thought discredit, depreciate, and even ostracize those who do not agree with them.

## SECRET ATHEISM

The speeches of Job's comforters expound the reasons that are periodically advanced today for the suffering of the righteous. Contemplate, first of all, a possible explanation by the messengers who brought to Job the news of his many disasters. According to the record, one messenger after another arrived and stoically broke to Job the news of his overwhelming losses, the loss of his property, the loss of his children, etc. It has been suggested that their stoical manner and attitude indicates that they may consider all of this wholly accidental. This represents much of the world's judgment today about the suffering and the troubles of the righteous. Men who do not know God eliminate Him from the scene of human action. Today, men of the world are practical atheists and fail to see God in current historical events. They feel that the universe is operated without a central governing Intelligence. This is the philosophy of humanism. But they are not alone in their feeling that God is remote—far off. Numerous believers doubt the immanence of God, that is, His continous ongoing participation in the affairs of men. It is tragic when the world loses its consciousness of God and His presence, thus creating virtual atheists. When this happens extensively, society goes berserk, and lawlessness, Godlessness, crime, and war sweep the nations. "Because sentence against an evil work is not executed speedily, therefore the heart of the sons of men is fully set in them to do evil" (Ecclesiastes 8:11). Men engage in evil when they relinquish their sense of God's omnipresence.

If men of the world were conscious that God is everywhere present, that they are accountable to a Supreme Being, it would act as a powerful inhibitor of evil tendencies. I am sorry to tell you that unbelievers are not alone in their notion that God is far off and that much that takes place in human experience has no explanation other than chance or accident. Even some ministers of the gospel seem to doubt the immanence of God. They cannot see Him active in human affairs. A basic reason for the position that the sufferings of the righteous are unaccountable and accidental is simply bland unbelief in an everpresent God, and that is merely concealed atheism. Here is the touchstone of all faith that is worthy of the name. The church, largely through the overexaltation of the human intellect, has permitted Satan to sterilize belief in the supernatural.

## ALMIGHTY LOVE REGULATES THE UNIVERSE

There was a time in my own life when I wondered, "Can it be possible that God is in all the little things of life?" I was born again and filled with the Spirit before I fully understood that God is omnipotent and omnipresent in His universe and that nothing escapes His notice. We learn from Proverbs 15:3 that "the eyes of the Lord are in every place, beholding the evil and the good." Psalm 139 teaches that we live in a totally transparent universe. It was years before I discovered that God is interested in *all* of our problems; that He is interested in everything that touches us; that "not a shaft can hit until His love sees fit." It was years before I learned that whenever I am sick or in need, God is at my elbow; that He suffers when I suffer. It was a long time before I learned that "in all of my affliction He is afflicted" (Isaiah 63:9). There can be no accidents in a world that is ruled by a God Who is omnipotent, omniscient, and omnipresent. A large number of theologically conservative ministers question the theology that breathes in the lines of John Greenleaf Whittier:

*I know not where His islands lift their fronded palms in air;*
*I only know I cannot drift beyond His love and care.*

Men who believe that the suffering of the righteous is purely accidental must question the beautiful theology of Whittier. In Hebrews 1:3 Paul says that "He (Christ) regulates the universe by the mighty power of His command." What a relief! There can be no accidents in a universe like that.

*No chance hath brought this ill to me;*
*'Tis God's own hand, so let it be,*
*He seeth what I cannot see,*
*There is a needs be for each pain;*
*And He one day will make it plain,*
*That earthly loss is heavenly gain.*
*Like as a piece of tapestry viewed from the back,*

*Appears to be naught but threads tangled*
*hopelessly;*
*But in the front a picture fair*
*Rewards the worker for his care,*
*Proving his skill and patience rare*
*Thou art the workman, I the frame,*
*Lord, for the glory of Thy Name,*
*Perfect Thine image on the same.*

Author unknown

INFINITE INTELLIGENCE IN CONTROL

It has previously been suggested that the stoical attitude of the messengers who reported the news of calamity to Job indicated their suspicion that these ill fortunes were purely accidental and without meaning. Countless numbers of us may see our faces in this mirror. When misfortune arrives, we sometimes say, "That is just part of life. We must expect such things. There is no rhyme or reason to life's circumstances. All is pure accident." But one who knew better wrote this line—"No chance hath brought this ill to me." To a good many people this seems an idiotic faith. And innumerable believers consider it to be wishful thinking. On the basis of the Word, we repeat that the incidents that came to Job and those that are coming to you are not accidents. *In the Book of Job we have a glimpse behind the scenes and we know that infinite intelligence was in control.* Today, the same God Who was active in Job's life is active in yours and mine as well. In a world ruled by an omnisicent, omnipotent, omnipresent God, in a world where the very hairs of your head are all numbered, in a world where not even a sparrow can fall without the Father's notice, there can be no accidents to a child of His love. When I went down with tuberculosis as a young man, the following profound lines were given to my mother, and she sent them to me while I was hopelessly ill in the Veteran's Bureau Hospital. At that time I could not see any motive, any purpose, any reason in my physical collapse. Everything seemed wrong. I was at the threshold of youth and broken for life. As I read these lines, I was full of skepticism and bitterness. For more than fifty-five years now, they have blessed and strengthened me. Perhaps they have a message for you.

*Behind my life, the Weaver stands,*
*And works His wondrous will:*
*I leave it in His all-wise hand,*
*And trust His perfect skill.*
*Should mystery enshroud His plan,*
*And my short sight be dim,*
*I will not try the whole to scan,*
*But leave each thread with Him.*
*Not till the loom is silent,*
*And the shuttles cease to fly,*
*Shall God unfold the pattern,*
*And explain the reason why*
*The dark threads were as needful*
*In the Master's skillful hand,*
*As the threads of gold and silver*
*In the pattern which He planned.*

Author unknown

GOD IS AT YOUR ELBOW

"The eyes of the Lord are in every place, beholding the evil and the good" (Proverbs 15:3). How can there be accidents in a world where "God never slumbers nor sleeps" (Psalm 121:3)? Turn with me to Psalm 139: "Whither shall I go from thy Spirit? Or whither shall I flee from thy presence? If I ascend into heaven, thou art there: if I make my bed in hell, behold, thou art there. If I take the wings of the morning, and dwell in the uttermost parts of the sea; even there shall thy hand lead me, and thy right hand shall hold me. If I say, surely the darkness shall cover me; even the night shall be light about me. Yea, the darkness hideth not from thee; but the night shineth as the day; the darkness and the light are both alike to thee." Do these words mean anything? If they do, they mean that God is everywhere. He is at your very elbow this present throbbing moment. You couldn't blink an eyelash without Him. However inscrutable God's providence may be, however mysterious His dealings with His saints, there can be no accidents in His world.

# SIX
# THE COMFORTERS GATHER

## THE DEFECTIVE THEOLOGY OF JOB'S FRIENDS

Most of us, like Job's friends, are better able to interpret the afflictions of others than our own. When they saw Job's condition, they were so shocked that for seven days and nights they were speechless. By the time Job finished his first complaint, they had had enough time to contemplate and philosophize concerning the reason for his affliction. They were obviously men of eminence, of high caliber. Their philosophical and theological insights were profound and logical. They were neither naive nor foolish. A sampling of their speeches indicates that there was much truth in their philosophy. They presented a very popular, conventional, and contemporary theology of suffering. But I am convinced it represented only one side of the coin. *They believed and taught that if one is wholly right with God, he will be delivered from all suffering, sorrow, calamity, or misfortune physically, materially, and socially. They believed that genuine integrity will be rewarded with earthly success, prosperity, and protection from difficulties of every kind.* They were positive that righteousness will be clearly authenticated, proved, and demonstrated by unbroken health, wealth, and happiness. If any of these is lacking it is because something is terribly wrong in the life of the sufferer. This is the conventional view of those who do not know why we are here or what for.

## THE BALANCING OF GOD'S BOOKS

*According to Job's friends, God balances His books in September.* If this were true, no one would have to wait for reward for righteousness or punishment for wrongdoing. It requires no faith to believe that it always pays to do right if the reward is immediate and instantaneous. If it is obvious that it always pays to serve God, faith would not be necessary. There would be no opportunity for faith to be tested and grow. If one always reaped the reward immediately for doing right or punishment for doing wrong, the incentive to do right and refrain from doing wrong would be wholly mercenary or selfish. *Moral values could not exist in such an order.* There is no moral value in the action of a person who removes his hand quickly from a red-hot stove. His motive is purely self-preservation. Likewise, there is no moral value in attending gospel worship on Sunday morning if one is hired and paid cash for doing so. *Also, there may be little moral and spiritual value in a healing where the sick person is not challenged to a new dimension of moral and spiritual dedication and is healed without making a spiritual adjustment.* A "presto chango" type of healing may be comfortable, but spiritually counterproductive. If Job had been healed without the new vision of God and the spiritual adjustment which he made, he would have been the loser. *Therefore, every affliction of a child of God is a call to a new dimension of spiritual exploration.*

*The universe is moral.* It is exactly the kind of universe God requires to select and train His eternal companion. This is why He does not balance His books in September. This may explain some divine delays. His delays are God's way of giving us time to grow, to hear His voice and make adjustments for growth in faith. *Normally God deals with the spirit before faith for the body increases and brings deliverance. Cleansing and growth in the spirit are God's primary aim and purpose in everything.* But Job's comforters didn't know this.

ELIPHAZ

Listen to Eliphaz: "Shouldn't you believe that God will care for those who are good? Have you ever known of a truly good and innocent person who was punished? Experience teaches that it is those who sow sin and trouble who harvest the same" (Job 4:6, 7, 8, *The Living Bible*). "My advice to you [Job] is this: Go to God and confess your sins to him" (Job 5:8, TLB). In both of these chapters Eliphaz insists that if a man is right with God he and his family will be kept from every kind of misfortune. Read the verses for yourself.

Again in chapter 15 he is openly judgmental of Job. "Have you no fear of God? No reverence for him? Your sins are telling your mouth what to say. Your words are based on clever deception" (verses 5, 6). "Even the heavens can't be absolutely pure compared to him! How much less someone like you, who is corrupt and sinful, drinking in sin as a sponge soaks up water" (verses 15, 16). In chapter 22, Eliphaz speaks a second time, "Is it because you are good that he is punishing you? Not all! It is because of your wickedness! Your sins are endless'' (verses 4, 5). The remainder of the chapter is full of similar accusations, with promises of prosperity for those who return to God and right their wrongs. Superficially this seems like excellent theology.

BILDAD

In chapter 8, Bildad speaks. In verse 3 he asks, ''Does God twist justice?'' In verses 6 and 7 he answers, ''If you were pure and good, he would hear your prayer, and answer you, and bless you with a happy home. And though you started out with little, you would end with much.'' In verse 20 he reasons, ''But look! God will not cast away a good man.''

Bildad is a ''long life and prosperity'' buff for religious professors. In chapter 18, verse 5 he further declaims, *''The truth remains that if you do not prosper, it is because you are wicked. And your bright flame shall be put out,''* (emphasis mine); that is, you shall have an untimely death.

ZOPHAR

In chapter 11 Zophar joins the chorus. In verse 6 he gives his opinion: ''Listen! God is doubtless punishing you far less than you deserve.'' In verses 13 and 14 he advises: ''Before you turn to God and stretch out your hands to him, get rid of your sins and leave all iniquity behind you.''

In his second speech, in chapter 20, Zophar returns to the attack: ''You have tried to make me feel ashamed of myself for calling you a sinner, but my spirit won't let me stop'' (verse 2). Through the remainder of the chapter he implies that as a sinner

Job actually "enjoys the taste of wickedness, letting it melt in his mouth" (verse 12). In verses 17 and 21 he accused Job of being a thief, and in verse 19, of oppressing the poor by foreclosing overdue mortgages. Job's three friends unanimously declared that Job's loss of health, wealth, and loved ones was the result of his premeditated and unconfessed sin. He was in trouble financially and was bereaved of loved ones for the same reason. God was punishing him for his wickedness.

S E V E N

# GOD IS THE JUDGE

## JOB'S DEFENSE

Job unhesitatingly answered them all by vigorous self-defense, demonstrating full confidence in his integrity. He categorically denied all guilt. He unblushingly said, "I am righteous" (Job 6:29, TLB). In 13:18 he repeats it emphatically: "I know that I am righteous." In 23:11 he amplifies his claim of innocence: "I have stayed in God's paths, following his steps. I have not turned aside." In 27: 5, 6, he continues his self-justification: "Until I die, I will vow my innocence. I am not a sinner—I repeat it again. My conscience is clear as long as I live."

In other passages he goes into detail to catalogue his charities, benevolences, and generous social services to widows and orphans and other underprivileged persons. He eulogizes his high moral standards in chapter 31:1 when he says: "I made a covenant with my eyes not to look with lust upon a girl." And in verse 9 he declares that he has never longed for another man's wife, because (verse 11) "Lust is a shameless sin, a crime that should be punished." Throughout this chapter Job pictures himself as a superior saint, the very soul of rectitude, moral purity and honor.

In the beginning of his trials Job weathered the storms of adversity with admirable faith and humility. But under the continuing pressure of unrelenting pain and the merciless accusations of his critics, it is no wonder that he vacillated between sublime heights of submission and faith and subterranean depths of doubt and despair.

After his initial losses, according to Job 1:22 "Job did not sin by charging God with wrongdoing" (NIV). Later, in his self-defense, as stated by Eliphaz, he implied that he was "more righteous than God and more pure than his Maker" (Job 4:17). Job's strong self-vindication led Bildad to ask: "Does God pervert justice?" In 19:6 and verses following, Job lapses into bitterness and says that God has wronged him and there is no justice. He has many brothers and sisters today who in sorrow, suffering, and pain have often been tempted to blame God for their misfortunes. Do any of you see your faces in this mirror?

## SATAN'S SECRET WEAPON

It seems that Job's comforters were probably Satan's secret weapon. A part of Satan's strategy was to so totally devastate Job that he would turn against God and become the enemy's trophy. His comforters carried on a constant barrage of vicious and unsupportable charges. A close study of Job's replies refutes the charges of defiance of God. Under unspeakable pressure Job apparently wavered. Admittedly he was thrown off balance, overwhelmed. But who wouldn't be? Mystified, yes! Tempted to rebellion, yes! But not to permanent alienation. *Perhaps no soul except Jesus was ever subject to such continuous, unrelenting, and massive assaults upon faith in God and his providences.* While Job maintained his integrity as a righteous man and resisted all attempts to brand him as an open sinner, *he did yield to the temptation to misjudge God.* Have not most of us been mystified by the inequities in the affairs of men and nations, and been tempted in the same way?

## JOB FALTERED

Like most of us, Job did fall short. He temporarily failed. In the midst of unprecedented satanic assaults, Job's faith did falter, yet in the darkest hours it rose to most sublime heights. In chapter 13:15 while his life hung in the balance, he gave the saints of all ages a monumental gem of faith. "Though he slay me, yet will I trust him." *The ultimate in faith may not be the faith that raises the dead but the faith that is based upon the character and integrity of God, rather than upon His performance.*

In another hour so dark that hope could not hear even the "rustle of a wing," his faith pierced the darkness with a breadth of vision that has comforted millions: "I know that my Redeemer lives, and that in the end he will stand upon the earth. And after my skin has been destroyed, yet in my flesh I will see God. I myself will see him with my own eyes—I, and not another" (Job 19:25-27, NIV).

Again, when silence was added to blackness, and God Himself seemed to be dead, Job recovered and refused to despair, "Behold, I go forward but he is not there; and backward, but I cannot perceive him; on the left hand, where he doth work, but I cannot behold him: he hideth himself on the right hand, that I cannot see him. But he knoweth the way that I take; when he hath tried me, I shall come forth as gold'' (Job 23:8-10, KJV).

## ELIHU

The last person to reply to Job was a man named Elihu. In chapter 36:8-14 (KJV) Elihu proclaims the principle that affliction may sometimes come as a moral and spiritual education, discipline, or child training. ''And if they be bound in fetters, or be held in cords of affliction; then he showeth them their works, and their transgressions that they have exceeded. He openeth also their ear to discipline, and commandeth that they return from iniquity.''

According to verse 7, these are good or righteous men Elihu is addressing. Therefore, he is not speaking of outbroken or premeditated sin. He evidently is thinking of faults, failures, or shortcomings resulting from the residual effects of the fall. He clearly teaches that affliction may come to enable upright people to hear God's instruction and grow in spiritual grace. In verses 15 and 16 Elihu says, ''But those who suffer he delivers in their suffering; he speaks to them in their affliction. He is wooing you from the jaws of distress to a spacious place free from restriction'' (NIV).

## A MODIFIED PHILOSOPHY

This philosophy is a distinct modification of that of the three previous speakers. It acknowledges that good men, even holy men, may need affliction to drive them to God, to facilitate their hearing His voice, to enable them to receive a new revelation of Him and, in that new light, a new revelation of their own unsuspected imperfections. *Even good men, holy men, if they take a light bright enough and go down deep enough into the subterranean caverns of their redeemed but fallen personalities, dispositions, and affections, may find there some slimy, crawling, malodorous traits, propensities, inclinations, or weaknesses of which they were previously totally unaware.* In some cases it could be the key to healing.

### NOT YET GLORIFIED

Because the crisis experience of the filling with the Spirit is not glorification, even a Spirit-filled person is still a fallen being. After grace has done its utmost, the residual effects of the fall remain to be disciplined, educated, and refined. Those negative effects consist of unlovely traits which progressively need the cross. The fall limits the positive graces of the Spirit such as love, joy, peace, longsuffering, gentleness, goodness, faith, meekness, temperance. They have a potential which only glorification will make possible. These graces will continue to increase throughout an endless eternity as we grow more and more into the sublime and transcendent beauty and likeness of our lovely Lord Jesus. "Beloved, now are we the sons of God, and it doth not yet appear what we shall be: but we know that, when he shall appear, we shall be like him; for we shall see him as he is" (1 John 3:2, KJV).

### AN INTERMEDIARY

Elihu claims that he stands as an intermediary between Job and God, the representative of both (Job 33:6, TLB). In 33:2-13 he points out that Job's sin was self-justification and judgmentalism against God. *Job's sin, therefore, was spiritual pride. This is the particular temptation and sin of the sanctified.* In the subsequent verses Elihu preaches a sermon on the methods God uses in communicating His mind and thought to those who are willing to listen. Among those methods are sickness and pain, sometimes so severe that the body wastes away and draws near to the gates of death (verses 14-30). But according to Elihu this affliction is remedial, for a messenger reaches the afflicted with the truth of a substitute and he is restored to health. Here, I believe, is a clear reference to the gospel of healing in the atonement, even in that early day. Elihu seems to agree that affliction comes with a message from the heart of God, and justifies God's use of adversity for teaching, training, and maturing spiritual life.

## GOD SPEAKS

Finally, God Himself confronts Job out of a whirlwind. In chapter 40, verse 8, God reminds Job of his sin of arrogance, unbrokenness, and self-righteousness: "Are you going to discredit my justice and condemn me so that you can say that you are right?" *Thus God exposes Job's sin as self-justification and spiritual pride.*

It is clear that while Job was not guilty of the gross sin of which his friends accused him, *he still needed a deeper brokenness and death. One of God's purposes in permitting Job's adversity was to give him a new revelation of God in order to disillusion him with himself. Disillusionment with one's self is an absolute necessity for further growth. All spiritual growth begins in self-disillusionment.* One of the great faults of mature sainthood is unconscious self-righteousness, unrealized self-exaltation. *It is easy for the most saint-*

*ly to fall prey to a superior estimation of his own spiritual state.* Satan aids and abets this tendency because it plays into his hands. This was Job's great problem. That is why he needed a deeper death.

## JOB'S SELF-DISILLUSIONMENT

By the time God finished speaking from the whirlwind, Job was speechless. He was totally and completely disenchanted and thoroughly humbled and subdued. In the light of God's self-revelation, Job saw himself and the residual corruption of his fallen nature for the first time. *Maclaren says that the closer one gets to God the more conscious he becomes of those things in his spirit, his disposition, and being which are not yet like God. Increasing light brings increasing sensitiveness to sin. Increasing sensitiveness of conscience is a sign of growing holiness just as increasing pain in a paralyzed limb is a sign of returning health.*

## SELF-ABHORRENCE: A HIGH STATE OF GRACE

Job's disillusionment with himself was the result of a new vision of the ineffable holiness of God and was followed by repentance and confession. His self-emptying was utter and profound: "*I have heard of thee by the hearing of the ear, but now mine eye seeth thee. Wherefore, I abhor myself and repent in dust and ashes*" (Job 42:5, 6, KJV). Regardless of the counselors and psychiatrists who seek to improve the self-image of their counselees, in the opinion of some, *this was the high-water mark of Job's experience. This is probably a higher state of grace than most of us achieve.*

Believe it or not, it appears that the judgmentalism of a fellow believer by Job's comforters was more offensive to God than Job's misjudgment of

God Himself. *In their judgmentalism Job's friends actually assumed God's prerogative.* In James 4:11, 12, (NIV), God unequivocally condemns judgmentalism of a brother believer. Notice this: "Brothers, do not slander one another. Anyone who speaks against his brother or judges him speaks against the law and judges it. When you judge the law, you are not keeping it, but sitting in judgment on it. There is only one Lawgiver and Judge, the one who is able to save and destroy. But you—who are you to judge your neighbor?" In God's sight their sin of self-righteousness and arrogance was greater even than Job's. They insisted that earthly prosperity always accompanies holiness and the lack of it is proof that the sufferer is guilty of gross outbroken sins. God seems to repudiate this philosophy and opts for the principle that the affliction of the righteous comes with a message from His heart. In Job's case, when he yielded to the chastisement and was willing to intercede for those who had wrongfully accused him, his fortunes turned.

## DOGMATISM OF JOB'S FRIENDS

Is it possible that the harsh, unloving criticism and judgmentalism of Job's friends of a fellow believer is more obnoxious to God than Job's misjudgment of God Himself? If we are to accept God's own appraisal, it would so appear. "After the Lord had said these things to Job, he said to Eliphaz the Temanite, 'I am angry with you and your two friends, because you have not spoken of me what is right [that is, the truth], as my servant Job has'" (Job 42:7, NIV). Their theology insisted that a right relationship with God will exempt one from sickness, sorrow, and suffering, both physically and materially. If a man is sick it is because he is a sinner, and he will be healed without fail when he acknowledges it. They preached that the measure of a person's sickness, poverty, and suffering indicates the measure of his guilt and wickedness, and that the dimension of his health, wealth, and success is an indication of the dimension of his holiness and righteousness. If a man really loves God, he will never be sick, and if he is sick he will be healed instantly if he accepts and practices their theology.

PARTIAL TRUTH

One cannot deny that there is partial truth in their theological positions. "Delight thyself in the Lord, and he will give thee the desires of thine heart" (Psalm 37:4, KJV). This is only one of the many passages in the Word that is a part of a beautiful gospel of health, wealth, and happiness for those who love the Lord. And all of them are true. But there are many passages which condition, modify, and supplement this theology. One ignores them at his peril. Paul reminds the Galatians that it was because of an illness that he first preached the gospel to them (Galatians 4:13). Some people believe, and there is some evidence, that Paul's thorn (2 Corinthians 12:7) was a physical affliction, but it served a valuable spiritual purpose. We believe that Satan could not touch Paul without God's permission, but God used the thorn to keep Paul from spiritual pride and exaltation. Very few of us have ever comprehended the enormity (in God's sight) of these sins. They caused Satan's fall.

They threaten every member of Christ's Body. God either had to limit Paul's revelation of God and heaven or permit the thorn. *Paul could not have the revelation without the thorn.* "To keep me from being conceited because of these surpassingly great revelations, there was given me a thorn in my flesh" (2 Corinthians 12:7, NIV). When Paul learned that God's power was made perfect in weakness and infirmity, he decided that he would prefer the "surpassingly great revelations" to the physical deliverance. The vast and overwhelming interest in physical healing today *may indicate that not everyone is as interested in spiritual growth as they are in health and comfort, and this may be one reason why some are not healed immediately.* May it also explain much shallowness of spiritual perception in the Church?

## GOD'S BEST CHOICE

Without doubt, health is God's first and best choice for *all* His people, *but he is more interested in spiritual health and maturity than He is in temporary physical comfort. In all of His dealing with us, God is working toward greater holiness.* If God sees that immediate and instantaneous restoration will best serve the purpose of spiritual health and maturity, then faith for immediate healing is probably always His will. If he has a new spiritual revelation for the sufferer, improvement may be delayed until greater growth.

## ALL BELIEVERS LEGALLY HEALED

*Every believer is legally healed clear up to glorification.* It is true that God has already done all He will ever do so far as provision for health is concerned. *Every believer was legally physically healed and even glorified at the cross.* "By whose stripes ye were healed" (1 Peter 2:24). This is a categorical statement from the Word of God. And Jesus Himself declared that the "Scripture cannot be broken" (John 10:35). *If this is accepted as true, then any symptoms that remain after the exercise of faith must only be to give us exercise in overcoming Satan and increasing rank in the ages to come.* "For those God foreknew he also predestined to be conformed to the likeness of his Son, that he might be the firstborn among many brothers. And those he predestined, he also called; those he called, he also justified; those he justified, he also glorified" (Romans 8:29, 30, NIV). *But only one man fully appropriated the legal provision of the all-sufficient atonement, and that was Enoch.* It is conceivable that what one man did by faith in the atonement others may do. *Since this is true, the fault for any failure of healing must be on the human side.* But this does not mean that if one is not healed it is because he is living in known sin. It only means that he is a fallen creature who, along with Abraham, Moses, and the prophets, did not attain faith to overcome all the effects of the fall. *Only Enoch reached this goal.*

## IMPORTANCE OF SPIRITUAL GROWTH

Strive to attain Enoch's faith, but if you do not, do not allow Satan to accuse, oppress, or defeat you because others are delivered from symptoms and you are not. Keep yielding, believing, and above all, keep growing. *To know that through the atonement one is legally delivered from every sickness and every disease is the basis and platform or staging area for mobilizing faith to appropriate that deliverance. The im-*

*portant thing is to grow. Growth in grace is so important to God that it may be the key to your healing. There is a very close relationship between growth in grace and the ability to exercise faith for healing.* Job was not healed in twenty-four hours. He had to grow in meekness, submission, and self-repudiation before healing faith was born. That could be your need as well. *To ignore the need for spiritual growth when praying for someone's healing may not fulfill God's highest purpose.* He is interested in your physical health, but He is supremely interested in your spiritual growth and development.

## DEFECTIVE THEOLOGY

The theology of Job's friends which God repudiated was not only a theology of health, it was also a theology of wealth and material prosperity. They believed and taught that if a man truly loves God, and if there is nothing wrong with his relationship with God, he will be healthy, wealthy and wise, and therefore prosperous and successful. There is a certain dimension of truth also in this theology. Holy living with its self-discipline, diligence, and high purpose has its economic advantages. "The drunkard and glutton shall come to poverty, and drowsiness shall clothe a man with rags" (Proverbs 23:21). Job's friends were sure that genuine piety and faith build a wall around a man so that he escapes all such calamities as ill health and poverty. *They taught that godliness gives a person a first mortgage on the Bank of Heaven.* There is much in the Word and elsewhere to support the faith that it is better in every way to serve God than the devil. Yet James reminds us that "God hath chosen the poor of this world to be rich in faith and heirs of the kingdom which he hath promised to those that love him'' (James 2:5).

KEY TO RESTORATION

In the opinion of some, the theology of Job's friends on health and prosperity, partially true though it is, is one-sided. God had something to say to Job through this affliction, but He also had something to say to Job's friends: ''After the Lord had said these things to Job, he said to Eliphaz the Temanite, 'I am angry with you and your two friends, because you have not spoken of me what is right, as my servant Job has''' (Job 42:7, NIV). *If Job's friends were right in their theology, the universe would not be moral.* There would be no opportunity for the testing and development of moral choice. If we understand what God is saying in this passage, He is totally rejecting the theology of Job's friends. If so, the Book of Job clearly endorses the position of Maclaren that every affliction comes with a message from God, and the proper approach to healing and financial prosperity is heart-searching, repentance, and confession as James advocates in James 5:16 (KJV): ''Confess your faults one to another and pray one for another, that ye may be healed. The effectual fervent prayer of a righteous man availeth much.'' *The fervent prayers of a righteous man may be ineffective if you are unwilling to become wholly transparent and confess your faults or sins to one another.* To be willing to say to husband or wife or church brother or pastor, ''The Lord has shown me that I was wrong in my spirit and attitude recently,'' or ''He has convicted me for my judgmentalism, criticism, or gossip,'' *this could be the key to restoration.* In some church divisions and disagreements, enough vitriol has sometimes been generated and demonstrated to choke a rattlesnake. Confession, restitution, and reconciliation may produce faith for healing and save a large doctor bill.

## THE SIN OF JUDGMENTALISM

Throughout the Book of Job God strongly condemns the sin of judgmentalism of a fellow believer. God showed His displeasure with the harsh criticism of Job by his friends. He was so displeased that He demanded that they offer sacrifices and seek Job's intercession in their behalf. The significance of this demand is easy to overlook.

Matthew 7:1 categorically forbids judgmentalism. Jesus said, "judge not." Judgmentalism has been defined as condemnation or unfavorable judgment or criticism of others because of their conduct or supposed motives or character. It is a critical evaluation of another person's inner being or worth. It is the most frequent cause of division and fragmentation of the Body of Christ. Disunity unquestionably causes more souls to be lost than any other sin. Therefore, we may some day discover that the love that covers, that prefers and honors one another, that wipes out judgmentalism and unites the Body in Christ is a greater miracle than opening blind eyes, deaf ears, or healing the lame so that they "leap as an hart."

If the salvation of a soul is the greatest miracle, then the love that unites the Body and paves the way for the salvation of souls may be a close second. Striving for and featuring sensational types of miracles may be less important in God's sight than seeking Body unity.

One cannot become judgmental without elevating himself, and self-elevation was Lucifer's syndrome. It caused his fall and all the sin and sorrow that followed and still follows in its wake. Satan could not be content to be second even to God Himself. This triggered his rebellion and the first broken fellowships in heaven. He infected the race with this virus. The mother tincture or essence of the fallen condition is self-exaltation, self-promotion, the determination to be first. Because too many of us want to be first and too few of us are willing to be last or even second, the Body remains broken and the hands of the Holy Spirit tied. Thus, the disposition of self-effacement, which is willing to humble itself and be last instead of first, is a greater miracle than walking on water. If we witnessed someone walking on water we would go wild with rejoicing. We would consider him worthy of high honor. May it not be that the miracle of all miracles of the church age is the *love that covers,* the love that is willing to be last that the Body may be united and the Holy Spirit released?

The Body made one as Jesus is one with the Father, every member "made perfect in one" with each other and the Godhead, this is the unanswered heart-cry of Jesus in John 17. *The absolute unity of the Body, the Church, would be the supreme miracle of the Church age,* not only because it overcomes human division, malice, and malevolence which is the hallmark of the fall, but because, as Jesus said, it is the most convincing testimony to the world that God has invaded the human scene. "That they all may be one; as thou,

Father, art in me, and I in thee, that they also may be one in us: that the world may believe that thou hast sent me'' (John 17:21-23, KJV).

Unity, love for one another, commanded by Jesus, is one thing that proves discipleship to the world. ''By this shall all men know that ye are my disciples, if ye have love one to another'' (John 13:35, KJV). It is the one thing that authenticates Christ's divinity and overcomes the world's unbelief. Unbelief is the world's chief sin, the sin that dooms all lost souls. And the chief sin of the Church is the lack of the love that covers. This love heals and unites the Body and is the supreme miracle of the Church age.

Only nonessentials to salvation can divide the Body because the true Church is united in all beliefs necessary to salvation. Otherwise the group calling itself the Church could not qualify as the real Body of Christ unless they accept all fundamental beliefs. Therefore, all divisions in the true Church must be over nonessentials. When irreconcilable opinions arise, what is the scriptural course of action? There are two options: One is to resort to lobbying to promote the preferred view. This often results in conflict, which gives rise to judgmentalism and greater broken fellowships. To resort to judgmentalism is always wrong because Christ has enjoined it, ''Judge not.'' Because Christ has said, ''Judge not,'' all judgmentalism has to be satanically inspired. This is Satan's method and always compounds the breach.

The second method is God's way and the only one that is effective. If a wrong has been done or an erroneous decision has been made which threatens division—*does God know it?* If I know a thing is wrong and needs to be corrected, does God also know? If God knows that an injustice has been done or a bad decision has been made that precipitates division, is He not as sincerely interested in its correction as I? Since He is the only One who can correct it, how will He do it? Not by my judgmentalism or party spirit, for that originates with Satan and is sure to exacerbate and aggravate the crisis. The only way that any situation, any situation which Satan has produced, can be rectified is by prayer, *for prayer is where the action is.*

"Prayer is the only thing that Satan cannot handle"—Jack Taylor. Because God has devised the plan of prayer primarily as on-the-job training for the Church in overcoming Satan in preparation for rulership in the ages to come, He does nothing except through prayer. If He went over the head of the Church and did the things He wants done without her cooperation in prayer, she would never learn overcoming. Even though all authority in heaven and in earth was given to Jesus, He has officially vested this hard-won authority over Satan in the members of His Body. Because such authority over Satan in earthly affairs has been delegated to her as His Body, *Christ Himself exercises no authority in mundane affairs over Satan and his hierarchy except through her prayer and faith.* Wesley said, "God does nothing except through prayer."

As the organic Head, He has voluntarily and for His own specific purpose limited the exercise of this authority to the members of His Body. It is hers and hers alone. She is His hands and feet. She is heaven's enforcement agency. Although all power and authority belongs to Him alone, it appears that since Christ's ascension and the birth of the

Church, He sovereignly chooses to exercise that earthly authority over Satan only through the Church, His Body, because this is the only way she learns overcoming. Jesus said in Luke 10:19: "Behold I give you power [authority] over all the power of the enemy . . . and nothing shall by any means hurt you." *This is a sweeping, official, constitutional, governmental decree charged with all the authority of heaven.*

The only power that can bind and cast out Satan is divine power, the power of the Holy Spirit. By God's own sovereign will that power is released solely by the prayer of the Church, but judgmentalism invariably paralyzes the spirit of prayer. Because judgmentalism which divides and separates the Body is a clear violation of Christ's command and always dims one's relationship with God, we know that it is spawned in hell and promoted by Satan. When a satanically inspired controversy arises in the Body, it can never be settled by lapsing into loveless judgmentalism. Because all judgmentalism is of the devil, it can never solve anything or anybody's problem. It is his tool, therefore, it can never heal any wound which it has caused. That would be like Satan casting out Satan. Only united prayer binds and casts Satan out. Through united prayer and faith, division will be overcome, wounds will be healed, the Body will be brought together, the world will be convinced, sinners will be saved, and Christ will be glorified. Where the love that covers prevails, Satan's techniques will be rejected, and prayer will supplant carnal methods.

Where *agape* love prevails, believing prayer will exercise God-given authority over Satan and his hierarchy. When the love that covers prevails and chooses the option of prayer over judgmentalism it provides convincing proof that prayer is where the action is. Any group or communion that practices this theology will discover that it works. Therefore, do not fall into Satan's trap of judgmentalism. Choose God's way, *the love that covers,* for love never fails, that is, its resources are ever all-sufficient.

# EIGHT
# JOB, THE DISCIPLINED SAINT

## JOB NEEDED FURTHER DISCIPLINE

We have followed Job from the depths of despair to the point where he began to see that his afflictions did have a purpose. We find that our experiences are often miniature replicas of Job's. In our own way, each of us who yields his life unreservedly into the hands of God, finds himself passing through the various stages, experiences, and discoveries concerning suffering through which Job passed. He finally reached a point where he could begin to understand something of the purpose of his afflictions. Although perfect in a relative sense, he still needed further discipline; he still needed refinement. And most of us do also. This viewpoint is often overlooked. Too many of us who feel that we are mature in grace fail to realize that God may yet have a controversy with something in our character or personality and that there may remain graces of the Spirit which God can add to us only through affliction.

One of the purposes of Job's suffering was to clarify his vision of God. No matter how well we know God, *there is always a deeper revelation, a clearer vision, a fuller understanding* that God may impart.

But this revelation may not be imparted without deep suffering and sorrow. This is unfolded in chapter 42:5: "I have heard of thee by the hearing of the ear; but now my eye seeth thee." God sought to bring Job into a more intimate life of fellowship with Himself, and *his deep afflictions were the means God used to realize His goal.*

## JOB NEEDED A DEEPER DEATH TO HIS RIGHTEOUS SELF

Another reason for Job's afflictions is revealed in his repentance. That was to bring him into a deeper death, even to his righteous self. After Job heard God speak in the whirlwind, he said, "I have heard of thee by the hearing of the ear; but now mine eye seeth thee. Wherefore I abhor myself and repent in dust and ashes" (Job 42:5, 6). When a saint can really see himself as God sees him and confess it, *that is a high state of grace.* Disillusionment with one's self is an absolute necessity for further growth. Believe me, beloved, *all spiritual growth begins in self-disillusionment.* A great fault of mature saints is self-righteousness, spiritual self-exaltation. To fall prey to a superior estimation of our own spiritual insight and judgment is easy, but fatal to growth. All spiritual leaders should beware of emasculating their message by self-complacency, arrogance, an attitude of superiority. *It is counterproductive to discredit, derogate, or unfavorably reflect upon the message of any other of God's servants. There is danger, beloved, that we who consider ourselves mature in grace may become the victims of unconscious spiritual pride.* That is a snare. And it is responsible for much shallow religious profession.

Some of the most mature saints have been the most conscious of shortcomings. They have been more suspicious of the corruption of their own nature than of others. *Just be sure of this, beloved, that the closer you get to God, the more conscious you will become of those things in your spirit which are not yet like God.* Job said, "I have heard of thee by the hearing of the ear: but now mine eye seeth thee." There was a new revelation of God first and then there was disillusionment with self. *Spiritual pride and arrogance cannot coexist with a new vision of the ineffable God. We need to remember that no matter how mature we may be, there are new heights and new depths of grace, new graces and virtues that await a new revelation of God.* If you live long enough and seek God earnestly enough, you may make this discovery for yourself. If we want God's best we will not allow imperfections to continue in our lives that will hinder His purpose for us.

## SATAN'S GREAT AIM—PREVENT SPIRITUAL GROWTH

Many of us are in Job's shoes and can see our faces in this mirror. He was totally unconscious of anything in his life with which God had a controversy. He was unconscious of any room for growth. He evidently was unaware that the biggest room in the world is the room for improvement and that this applies to one's spiritual life. *The human spirit, created in the image and likeness of God, is the most sublime and exalted entity in the universe next to God.* It is so vast, its potentialities are so voluminous, that after one has grown a million years, he will have as much spiritual progress to make as when he was first born again. *Because the character of Jesus is infinite, those advanced in grace have as much to learn as the beginner.* If you ever had any question about what you will be doing in eternity, give this a thought: Approximating the infinite beauty of Jesus means infinite growth. Satan's great aim is to prevent growth. He wants every believer to be stunted now, just where he is.

Some teachers will be appalled at this, but each new vision of God reveals to the believer vast new divine potential for growth in Christlikeness. Christ's message to the Laodicean Church in Revelation 3 exposes all complacency and self-satisfaction as of the devil because it halts growth immediately. *If God gave us faith for healing before we took the next step in growth, we would probably not take that step and we would be the loser. Spiritual growth is more important in God's sight than a comfortable body.*

### SPIRITUAL GROWTH— ITS RELATIONSHIP TO HEALING FAITH

*Because of the inertia of the fallen nature, spiritual growth would reasonably cease or be greatly retarded without the experience of adversity. If God gave faith for perfect healing and health in every sickness without delay, at the first cry, it is doubtful that we would seek Him as we do when in sickness and pain.* This was demonstrated in Israel's experience. "Whenever God slew them, they would seek him; they eagerly turned to him again. They remembered that God was their Rock, that God Most High was their Redeemer" (Psalm 78:34, 35, NIV). And are we not all in the same boat as inconstant Israel? Could variations in growth and in our response to chastening be a reason why some receive faith for healing and others do not? Or why some receive faith for healing in some but not all afflictions? Because growth in grace (2 Peter 3:18) is so indispensable to God, there may be a close relationship between growth and faith for healing.

## SPIRITUAL INFECTION—FAITH FOR HEALING

To be miraculously healed in a healing service by the exercise of gifts of healing without spiritual growth, if that were possible, may be little different from magic or healing by the occult. *Healing of the body that is divine is primarily a spiritual work, because God is more interested in the healing of the spirit than in the healing of the body.* The spirit is the real person, and that is what God is after. We may some day discover that a seemingly slight infection in one's spirit may be sufficient to prevent faith for healing. James acknowledged this when he said, "Confess your faults one to another, that ye may be healed" (James 5:16). *We may also discover that unholy attitudes such as self-pity, ill-temper, resentment, lack of consideration for others, and judgmentalism of one another in the Church, home, or community may be sufficient to hinder exercise of faith for healing. The distemper of the spirit may be reflected in a physical affliction because it prevents the free exercise of faith.* The Holy Spirit is sensitive to our humors, even our moods, if they are influenced by the flesh. It may be that disagreeableness, harshness or lack of consideration for a mate may betray a plague spot in disposition which obstructs the free flow of faith for the healing of body. May it not be "the little foxes" (Song of Solomon 2:15) which spoil the vine that produces the fruit of faith? This is not a contradiction of the so-called faith message. This seeks to remove the hindrances to faith. There are two sides to faith and both are equally valuable. It is not either/or; it is both/and.

## GOD USED JOB'S "FRIENDS"

Perhaps even more responsible determinatives are the broken fellowships, lack of forgiveness, and the grudges which sometimes exist in the spirits of those seeking physical wholeness. As I said before, some who profess a high state of grace demonstrate enough vitriol in their spirits to choke a rattlesnake. Broken fellowships, including suits in court, by spiritual leaders even in world-famous organizations are an example. But God was using Job's friends all the while to prepare Job for "twice as much." The people who are most congenial to us may not be as good for our spiritual growth as those who irritate us. *If our reaction is right, those who irritate or antagonize us may offer a more positive opportunity for growth in* agape *love and eternal rank.* We cozy up to those who soothe our ego, those who agree with us, those we can use to advance our goals. This often merely enlarges one's ego and usually diminishes one's capacity to love. *The graces of the Spirit grow mainly through exercise and testing. God used the severe judgmentalism of Job's friends to produce a deeper death to himself.*

## JOB'S GREAT TEST

After God's confrontation with Job and his repentance, Job faced a monumental test. After a long period of unprecedented vilification in which he was driven to wish for death, after accusing him of the most dastardly deeds, after, as tools of Satan, they viciously slandered him, they came to Job seeking his pardon. Job had suffered under satanic pressures as perhaps no one except Jesus ever did. If Job had not been so thoroughly disillusioned with himself, so totally broken and humbled, it is doubtful if he could have met this test of forgiveness. It would have been most natural for him to refuse pardon. God demonstrated His interest in the love that covers and forgives by healing Job and restoring his fortune when he forgave and prayed for his friends. *This demonstrates God's longing for the unity of His Body as set forth in John 17.*

## THE GREATEST SIN OF THE CHURCH

*Because it causes more souls to be lost, the greatest sin of the Church is probably the sin of disunity, broken fellowships, unforgiveness, and resentment.* At times we try to hush things and paper over controversies without ventilating and healing them. At times physical wounds need to be opened and irrigated before they will heal. It often is similar in spiritual injuries. God showed His approval of the way of perfect transparency in the case of Job and his friends. *Before Job could pray effectively for his friends, he had to forgive them from his heart. No one can pray successfully while holding a grudge.* The evidence that Job's forgiveness and reconciliation was full and complete is the fact that Job was healed and his fortunes restored and that his friends were also healed.

The disciples' prayer points up the revelance of forgiveness and unity. Jesus revealed that God is very sensitive about our attitudes toward each other in His comment that unless they forgive those who sinned against them, God would not forgive the disciples themselves (Matthew 6:14, 15).

## JOB'S CAPTIVITY TURNED

The reason God is so deeply interested in our forgiving and loving one another is very simple. As Creator, He loves all of His intelligent creation equally. The person who has crossed swords with you or who has offended or injured you is just as dear to the Father as you are. Jesus shed His blood for him as truly as for you. God has just as great an investment in the one you are tempted to reject as He has in you. All are equally precious to Him no matter how they may have wounded you. You should remember that *you may also be guilty of wounding others.* This is why God demands that he who loves God love his brother also (1 John 4:21), because we cannot truly love Him who begat, and hate the one who is begotten of Him. We cannot love the Father without loving His Son also. This is why God strongly desires us to love and forgive each other. *This is why God turned the captivity of Job when he prayed for his friends.*

Lack of generosity, harshness, unlovingness toward a brother, sister, or mate may be enough to cripple faith for healing. "Beloved, let us love one another; for love is of God" (1 John 4:7). *A negative attitude toward another, toward pastor, husband, wife, or a brother in the Church may be sufficient to insulate or shortcircuit the connection with power.* This may explain why some are not healed.

## UNSUSPECTED EVIL

Dr. Henry Thiessen, in his little book on Job, has this to say: "The more consciously a soul walks in the presence of God the more deeply does it apprehend its own inborn corruption." Paul discovered that in him, that is in his flesh, there dwelt no good thing; for while to will was pr with him, he did not find how to perform that which was good. He came to look upon his inner corruption as "this body of death." In his *Imitation of Christ*, Thomas a Kempis says: "He that knoweth himself well is vilest in his own sight and hath no delight in man's praise."

Here are some significant lines from Fénelon, the great medieval mystic: "Nothing is really great except lowliness . . . detachment from one's own opinion and will . . . . All stiff, harsh goodness is contrary to Jesus Christ." Fénelon, as one of the most illustrious saints since the apostolic age, further affirms, "It is no wonder that, as your inward light grows clearer, the imperfections in yourself, which you had seen only dimly, should be revealed to you in their full strength and malignity; or that the evil should appear whose very existence in your heart you had never suspected."

Once the full light of God's presence is consciously turned on, one may uncover a measure of pride, jealousy, selfishness, hate, uncleanness, etc., in his own heart of which he was previously totally unaware. *Often one cannot be brought into this consciousness apart from afflictions.*

IMPORTANCE OF CONFESSION

Job not only said, "I abhor myself and repent in dust and ashes," but he humbly, openly confessed his need. Here is where advanced or mature believers often fail. Even after the works of grace in sanctification, cleansing, and the filling with the Spirit, some of us find it about as difficult to confess and go back on our faults as the sinner does to confess his open sins and go back upon himself.

We find it difficult to be as honest with our own hearts before God as we expect sinners to be. And this may be one reason why more sinners are not ready to confess, because some of us who profess the name of the Lord Jesus Christ are not willing to confess our needs. We exhort sinners to confess and forsake their sins, but we are very slow to confess our shortcomings and faults and make adjustments. Thus we believe that God may have a purpose in the afflictions of those who are particularly advanced in grace, and that is to work a deeper death in them to themselves and their estimated spiritual superiority.

Following is a verbatim extract from a copy of a letter from Mrs. Susannah Wesley to her son Charles. It appeared in the *Wesleyan Advocate* of July 22, 1974. The *Wesleyan Advocate* is the official organ of the Wesleyan Church. Here is part of Mrs. Wesley's reply to her son Charles' censorious letter in which he sharply criticized his mother and even called her Christian experience into question:

"I thank you for your kind letter. I call it so, because I do verily believe it was dictated by a sincere desire of my spiritual and eternal good. There is too much truth in many of your accusations nor do I intend to say one word in my own defense . . . But this I must tell you, you are somewhat mistaken in my case, alas! It is far worse than you apprehend it to be. I am not one of those which have never been enlightened or been made partaker of any heavenly gift, or of the Holy Ghost, but I have many years since been fully awakened and deeply sensible of sin both original and actual. But my case is rather like that of the Church at

Ephesus. I have been unfaithful in the talents committed to my trust and have lost my first love."

Here is an example of the humility of this mother of John and Charles Wesley, the originators of the Wesleyan doctrine of holiness. Should it not shame all followers of Wesley, including advocates of the full gospel, out of the spiritual pride and arrogance which sometimes mars and limits "our" ministry?

## PURPOSES OF AFFLICTION

Let us review some of the purposes and results of affliction as divulged in the life of Job. First, there was a new vision of God. "I have heard of thee by the hearing of the ear; but now mine eye seeth thee." Second, there was a deeper death to the natural self-life. Even the good self had to die. "Wherefore I abhor myself, and repent in dust and ashes." Another purpose of Job's affliction was to enlarge the sufferer's prosperity. The Psalmist says: "Thou hast enlarged me when I was in distress" (Psalm 4:1). In Job's case we read, "Also the Lord gave Job twice as much as before. Then came there unto him all his brethren, and all his sisters, and all they that had been his acquaintances before, and did eat bread with him in his house: and they bemoaned him, and comforted him of all the evil that the Lord had brought upon him: every man also gave him a piece of money, and everyone an earring of gold. So the Lord blessed the latter end of Job more than the beginning: for he had 14,000 sheep, and 6,000 camels, and 1,000 yoke of oxen, and 1,000 she asses. He also had seven sons and three daughters . . . and in all the land were no women found so fair as the daughters of Job: so Job died, being old and full of days'' (Job 42:10-13, 15, 17, KJV).

## ADVERSITY BEFORE PROSPERITY

God had twice as much for Job in mind from the very beginning. He wanted to prepare Job for greater prosperity. *We may not be ready for prosperity until we have been prepared by adversity.* Before God can trust us with prosperity, He must make us suitable for it. The man that cannot stand adversity may be unable to stand prosperity. *Prosperity may be a greater strain upon character than adversity.*

Although the atonement covers the entire scope of human need, God may have to fit us for prosperity by strange providences, by disappointments, frustrated ambitions and desires, and failures in undertakings as He did in the case of Job. Occasionally, as in Job's situation, He may train us with sickness, sorrow, bereavement, and pain. *It is always safe to say that when a saint is passing through a heavy trial, God is aiming at twice as much as before.* We may make the same mistakes as Job's friends and say that the saint is being punished, but that is probably incorrect. *The adversity of a saint is never punishment.* A saint may be chastened—he may be educated—he may be perfected—but he is not being punished, unless he loses patience, rebels, and ceases to be a saint.

A saint may suffer because of his shortcomings, faults, or failures, or because he is being perfected for something superior. *Every chastisement is both a command and a promise; a command to put off more of the self-life, even the legitimate self-life, and a promise of twice as much as we had before, when we obey.* As the

Psalmist said, "Thou has enlarged me when I was in distress."

## PREPARATION FOR PROSPERITY

Quoting again from Dr. Thiessen: "From all this we learned a lesson, that affliction is intended by God to prepare us for greater prosperity. Most of us cannot bear great prosperity; we tend to say that our wisdom and strength have brought it to us. Therefore, it is often necessary for God first to bring us very low, before He can lift us up."

## ALL FLESHLY ACTIVITY—COUNTERPRODUCTIVE

We need to reach the place where with Paul we have absolutely no confidence in our flesh. *Many of us do not know that in the realm of the spiritual, any activity of the flesh is counterproductive.* This is because we forget that *agape* love is the most powerful force in the universe. If God's method of *agape* love seemingly fails to achieve our desires, we are in danger of lapsing into the flesh. *No spiritual victory is won and no spiritual progress is made by giving way to the flesh.* In Philippians 3:3, Paul says, "It is we who are the circumcision, we who worship by the Spirit of God, who glory in Christ Jesus, and who *put no confidence in the flesh.*" (Emphasis mine.) *One may exercise authority over Satan only to the degree that he is delivered from confidence in the flesh.*

When we succumb to the use of fleshly methods, we are under Satan's leadership; we have yielded to his suggestion and adopted his methods. We do this only when we suspect, consciously or unconsciously, that Satan's method is more efficient than God's. This is why nothing of spiritual value can be accomplished by the flesh. It is possible to drop into the flesh even after we have been filled with the Spirit. We often do when we cannot get our way otherwise. This is defeat. To operate by fleshly methods, by the power of our own personality, gifts, or talents, or the use of psychology, human force, fleshly persuasion, cleverness, loss of temper, harshness, haste, impetuosity—these and all other activities of the carnal man are counterproductive in the spiritual realm.

*If the flesh is more effective than* agape *love, would not God be using it and its methods? To believe in and adopt Satan's methods, to place confidence in earthly wisdom, to believe that Satan's way of human might is more efficacious and successful, more powerful than God's way of* agape *love, is to believe that Satan himself is more powerful than God. This means he has deceived us as he did Eve and one-third of the angels and as he has deceived the whole world, even some spiritual leaders.*

If we believe that God is God and that love is the most potent force in the universe, we will be governed by it in our personal relationships with one another in the home, church, and the social order, because we are convinced that living after our old Adam is less effectual than walking in the Spirit. This is why Paul says in Romans 8:8, "So then they that are in the flesh cannot please God." This is because Paul knew that natural creature activity just doesn't work in the realm of the Spirit. We profess to be Spirit-filled, but do we continue to operate by the life of nature and self? *The point is not that if we are really filled with the Spirit we will walk in the Spirit, but that if we do not walk in the Spirit we are counterproductive even if we have been filled with the Spirit. The question is, "Where is our faith? In God or*

*Satan?"* Reliance on the wrong method accounts for most of our troubles which arise from unbrokenness, the fact that our flesh has not been totally subdued.

## SUBDUED

George D. Watson has penned these great words:

> Before God can launch us out into the breadth and sweetness of His service, and entrust to us great things for Himself, we must be perfectly subdued in every part of our nature to His will, and the disposition of His mind. We must be subdued in our hearts, in our wills, in our words, in our tempers, and in our manners; subdued through and through so thoroughly that we will be flexible to all his purposes and plans. We must be so subdued that harshness, severity, criticism, sluggishness, laziness, impetuosity, and all wanting our own way, even in religious matters, must be subdued out of us. Conversion will not finish this work, and perhaps in not one case in a thousand will the second work of grace produce this complete condition of teachable subjugation to God's Spirit.
>
> We must be subdued, not merely in our own opinions, not merely think ourselves subdued; not only be subdued in the esteem of our friends and fellow workers, but subdued so perfectly that the all-seeing eye of God can look us through, and the Omniscient One knows that we are subdued. *God must conquer the man He can trust with His great thoughts and plans.* [Emphasis mine.]

The Holy Ghost must saturate us with a divine conquest before He can use us to conquer other souls. The Lord will begin to subdue us with gentle means, and, if we sink lovingly and promptly into His mind, the work will be done, but if we have flint and iron in our nature, and it is necessary, He will use heroic means, and put us between the millstones and grind us to powder, until He can mould us without any resistance to His purpose. The greatest difficulty in the way of God's best servants, even His zealous and oftentimes sanctified servants, is that they are not perfectly and universally and constantly subdued under the power of God.

We must be so subdued as to stop meddling with other people's matters that God has not entrusted us with; so subdued as not to be calling God's servants hard names, and thrusting at Christians who are doing what they can in their various fields for the Master; so subdued that we can hold our tongues and walk softly with God, and keep our eyes upon Jesus, and attend to our own work, and do God's will promptly, lovingly, glad to have a place in His kingdom and do a little service for Him. Oh, it is grand to be *absolutely* conquered by the Holy Ghost, and swing out a thousand miles from everybody and everything into the ocean of God's presence and work with Him in humility, without chafing, without faultfinding, without stumbling over others, without religious peevishness, and bend with every plan that God gives to us.

If we do not love God supremely when prosperity comes, we will lavish its values and substance upon ourselves and forget the Giver. This is true not only of larger material blessings, but wonder of wonders, also of larger spiritual blessings. How many a servant of God has come to his ruin through prosperity in Christian service! Superficially, many of us would think that no amount of spiritual blessing could damage anyone. But how many people we know who have been used tremendously of God at some period in their lives, have grown eminent, famous, and affluent, and through their spiritual prosperity they have become exalted, lifted up, and vulnerable for a fall. And how great has been the fall of some mighty men of God! How many a person who was used of God in early life has been covered with a cloud of darkness and disgrace at the end of life, as Solomon was, for example. Hezekiah's biggest failure came after the biggest miracle of his experience, his healing and the promise of the fifteen-year extension of his life. It may be a short distance from immense spiritual blessing to the self-exaltation that produces a fall. *Spiritual blessings may indeed be hazardous to the soul that is not prepared first of all by adversities.* Dr. Thiessen says: "Let us, therefore, welcome the training of God in the school of suffering in order that we may become qualified for the greatest spiritual prosperity!" Maltie Babcock has said: "The tests of life are to make—not to break us. Trouble may demolish a man's business but build up his character. The blow at the outward man may be the greatest lesson to the inner man. If God then puts or permits anything hard in our lives, be sure that the real peril, the real trouble is what we shall lose if we flinch and rebel."

*Heroes are forged on anvils hot with pain,*
*And splendid courage comes but with a test.*
*Some natures ripen and some natures bloom*
*Only on blood-wet soil, some souls prove great*
*Only in moments dark with death or doom.*

Author unknown

GOD'S AIM—TWICE AS MUCH

*Before God could give Job twice as much as he had before, he had to make him twice as humble, twice as meek, and twice as lowly of mind. God deals with all of us in the same way and for the same purpose.* We cry out that He is breaking us when He is only making us adaptable for twice as much as before. Everything in God's order is directed toward the enlargement of a saint's character, the enlargement of his moral and spiritual resources. In order to attain this, God has to be willing many times, Himself, to be misjudged and misunderstood. One of the evidences of God's love for us is just this—that He is willing to be misunderstood by the one He is seeking to bless and enrich. Job said, "Though He slay me, yet will I trust Him," and while he waited, strangely enough, life advanced by its very contradictions and was enlarged by its restrictions and fertilized by its losses.

*One of our major difficulties is to accept partially understood providences.* But all the while God was dealing with Job, He was equipping him for the perils of prosperity. Job received twice as much as he had before because he was twice as mature and trustworthy. Listen: "I abhor myself and repent." That is where a man must be before God can fully trust him. Be sure of this, that God will see that we get all that is coming to us. *When we are ready for a throne, He will have the throne ready for us.*

*Please consider this study of the Book of Job as incomplete. Limited space and insufficient maturity prohibit full treatment of many important segments.*

*P.E.B.*